D0013951

Life-Enriching Education
Nonviolent Communication Helps Schools Improve Performance,
Reduce Conflict, and Enhance Relationships.
Copyright © 2003 by Marshall B. Rosenberg, Ph.D.

Requests for permission should be addressed to:

PuddleDancer Press, Permissions Dept.,
P.O. Box 231129, Encinitas, CA 92023-1129
Fax: 1-858-759-6967 Email: email@PuddleDancer.com

Author: Marshall B. Rosenberg, Ph.D.
Editor: Kathy Smith
Project Director: Jeanne Iler
Index: Phyllis Linn, INDEXPRESS
Cover and Interior Design: Lightbourne

Manufactured in the United States of America

ISBN: 1-892005-05-0

Library of Congress Cataloging-in-Publication Data

Rosenberg, Marshall B.
   Life-enriching education : nonviolent communication helps schools improve performance, reduce conflict, and enhance relationships / by Marshall B. Rosenberg.-- 1st ed.
      p. cm.
   ISBN 1-892005-05-0
   1. Teacher-student relationships. 2. Affective education. 3. Communication in education. I. Title.
   LB1033.R66 2003
   371.102'2--dc21
                              2003011055

Life-Enriching Education

Education

Nonviolent Communication Helps Schools
Improve Performance, Reduce Conflict,
and Enhance Relationships.

Marshall B. Rosenberg, Ph.D.

PuddleDancer PRESS

P.O. Box 231129, Encinitas, CA 92023-1129
email@PuddleDancer.com • www.PuddleDancer.com

Acknowledgments

I am grateful to master teacher Bill Page for giving me, more than 30 years ago, the opportunity to clarify how I would like to see teachers and students working together.

I am also grateful to JoAnne Anderson and Tom Shaheen, school administrators in Rockford, Illinois at that time, for giving me the chance in the late 1960s to participate with them in creating schools that functioned in harmony with my values.

These experiences along with the writings of John Holt, Ivan Illich, John Gatto, and Alfie Kohn deepened my awareness of the politics of education, and further increased my hunger to contribute to radical changes in education. More recently, Riane Eisler' writings on partnership and dominator education have been influential in this context.

How grateful I am also to my colleagues Miri Shapiro in Israel, Nada Ignjatovic in Serbia, Vilma Costetti in Italy, and Rita Herzog in the United States for demonstrating what each of us can do to transform schools that teach Domination into schools that provide Life-Enriching learning opportunities.

And finally I would like to express deep gratitude to Kathy Smith, with additional help from Rita Herzog and Gary Baran, for editing what I have written and translating my university English into readable English.

Contents

Acknowledgements • ix

Foreword by Riane Eisler • xi

Author's Foreword • xv

CHAPTER 1: TOWARD LIFE-ENRICHING EDUCATION • **1**

Introduction • 1

Life-Enriching Organizations • 1

Life-Enriching Education • 3

Changing the System • 4

NVC in Education—Sharing the Field • 5

CHAPTER 2: EXPRESSING LIFE-ENRICHING MESSAGES • **11**

Preparing Students • 11

The Effects of Moralistic Judgments on Learning • 12

Performance Evaluation Using Value Judgments • 14

Components of Nonviolent Communication • 15

Making Clear Observations Without Mixing in Evaluations • 16

Exercise 1—Observation or Evaluation? • 20

Identifying and Expressing Feelings • 23

Exercise 2—Expressing Feelings • 26

The Risks of Not Expressing Our Feelings • 29

Exercise 3—Acknowledging Needs • 33

Requesting That Which Would Make Life More Wonderful • 36

The Difference Between Requests and Demands • 38

Exercise 4—Expressing Requests • 40

The Process is the Objective • 43

People Can Hear Demands No Matter What We Say • 44

NVC in Education—Fun For Everyone • 47

CHAPTER 3: HEARING MESSAGES WITH EMPATHY • 51

Empathy • 51

Verbally Reflecting What We Hear • 53

Listening for Requests • 54

Connecting Empathically • 55

Empathically Connecting With Others When They Don't
Know How to Express Themselves or Choose Not To • 59

*Exercise 5—Differentiating Between Receiving
Empathically And Non-Empathically • 63*

**CHAPTER 4: CREATING PARTNERSHIP RELATIONSHIPS
BETWEEN TEACHERS AND STUDENTS • 67**

Partnership in Setting Objectives and Evaluation • 67

Objectives with Life-Enriching Purposes • 68

Students Have Always Had a Choice • 70

Teachers Fears of Student Involvement in Objective Setting • 71

Examples of Mutual Objective Setting • 72

Hearing the Need Behind the "No." • 74

Exercise 6—Hearing the Need Behind "No" • 77

The Most Important Part of Learning • 81

Students Fears of Student Involvement in Objective Setting • 82

Partnership in Evaluation • 83

Accountability, "Yes," Grades, "No" • 87

NVC in Education—The Test • 91

**CHAPTER 5: CREATING AN INTERDEPENDENT
LEARNING COMMUNITY • 97**

Secular Ethics • 97

Developing an Interdependent Learning Community • 98

The Teacher as a Travel Agent • 100

Materials That Allow Students to Learn by Themselves • 101

Utilization of Students and Parents in Providing Materials • 102

Volunteer Tutoring Services • 103

The Geographical Community as a Learning Resource • 104

The Travel Agent in Action • 104

CHAPTER 6: TRANSFORMING SCHOOLS • 109

The Problems at Hand • 109

Domination Organizations • 109

Conflict Resolution • 111

Mediation • 118

NVC in Education—"You're Dead" • 120

Avoiding Moralistic Judgments and Diagnoses • 126

Protective Use Of Force • 128

Exercise 7—Protective Use of Force vs. Punitive Use of Force • 131

Creating Sustaining Teams • 135

Transforming Our Schools • 138

Bibliography • 141

Index • 149

Note pages • 155

Some Basic Feelings and Needs We All Have • 161

About CNVC and NVC • 162

Trade Publications Available from PuddleDancer • 164

Booklets Available from CNVC by PuddleDancer • 166

The Compassionate Classroom • 167

CDs and Cassettes Available from Sounds True • 168

Center for Nonviolent Communication Materials Order Form • 169

About the Author • 171

How you can use the NVC Process • (back inside cover)

Foreword by Riane Eisler

M any of us recognize that fundamental change in education is urgently needed. We recognize that most present educational systems are not preparing children to meet the unprecedented challenges of the 21st century. We recognize that real educational reform is essential if today's and tomorrow's children are to live in a more peaceful, just, and sustainable world.

In this book, Marshall Rosenberg describes key elements of what he calls life-enriching education: an education that prepares children to learn throughout their lives, relate well to others and themselves, be creative, flexible, and venturesome, and have empathy not only for their immediate kin but for all of humankind.

Enriching life—expanding our minds, hearts, and spirits—should be the goal of education. Unfortunately, traditional education has often constricted rather than expanded the human mind, heart, and spirit. It has interfered with our natural curiosity and joy in learning, suppressed inquisitiveness and critical thinking, and modeled uncaring and violent behaviors.

Fortunately, today most Western schools no longer use violence against children, as in the old motto "spare the rod and spoil the child." But they still use other teaching methods designed to prepare people to unquestioningly obey orders from above—be it from their teachers in school, supervisors at work, or rulers in government.

The curriculum, also, often presents violence and domination as normal, even desirable—as in history classes where children must memorize the dates of battles and wars, and literature classes where they are assigned epics in which violent conquest is idealized as manly and heroic. The structure of schools itself is also generally still one of top-down rankings in which education is something done to students rather than with students.

This type of educational process, content, and structure is appropriate for what I have called the dominator or domination model of society—where families, workplaces, tribes, and states are organized into rigid rankings of domination ultimately backed up by fear and force. It is not an education appropriate for democratic, equitable, and peaceful societies—societies orienting to what I call the partnership model, and Rosenberg calls a life-enriching structure.

Obviously there has already been considerable movement away from the domination model, at least in some world regions. Had there not been, we could not be talking of fundamental educational change without risking severe consequences, even death—as was the case for any free thought and speech not so long ago during the European Middle Ages, and is still the case in many places today.

But this forward movement has not been linear. It has not only been fiercely resisted every step of the way; it has also been punctuated by regressions to the domination model. We are experiencing such a regression worldwide today—a regression to more, rather than less, inequality, violence, and human and environmental exploitation and domination. This is why the application of Rosenberg's Nonviolent Communication methods to education is so important, so urgent, and so timely.

Marshall Rosenberg is known worldwide as a pioneer in nonviolent conflict resolution. He has dedicated the last forty years of his life to developing and applying Nonviolent Communication as a tool for relations in which each person is treated with empathy and caring. In this book, he shows us how to use this method in schools. He also shows its effectiveness in preparing young people to work together, resolve conflicts nonviolently, and contribute to both their own and others' well-being in empathic and caring ways.

One of the most notable characteristics of Rosenberg's work is this focus on caring, empathy, and nonviolence—characteristics that in domination-oriented cultures are relegated to those who are excluded from social governance: women and "effeminate" men. Marshall recognizes that these are precisely the characteristics we have to nurture in both boys and girls, and shows how we can do this through tested and effective educational methods that allow young people to experience partnership in action.

This experience is important for all children. When children experience the life-enriching partnership relations Marshall describes in this book, they flourish. Experiencing these relations is particularly important for children who have in their homes, neighborhoods, and/or nations learned only two alternatives: you either dominate or you are dominated. It shows them that there is another alternative that feels and works much better for everyone.

Schools in which students and teachers relate as partners—where Marshall's nonviolent life-expanding education is part of every interaction—are communities of learning rather than top-down, impersonal factories. Young people begin to see school as a place of exploration, a place to share feelings and ideas, a safe and exciting place where each child is recognized and valued and the human spirit is nurtured and grows.

And there is more. When we give young people the opportunity to experience relations based on mutual respect and caring, we not only promote their well-being, learning, and personal growth. We also support the shift to a less violent, more equitable, caring, and truly democratic society.

In our age of nuclear and biological weapons, humanity stands at an evolutionary crossroads. At our level of technological development, the chronic violence and lack of caring and empathy required by relations conforming to the domination model threaten our very survival.

On one side lies the road of regression to even more rigid domination—familial, educational, religious, economic, and political.

On the other side lies the road to a more equitable, less violent, more caring partnership future. The movement toward partnership has been escalating for several centuries, partly due to the destabilization of habits and institutions by the technological changes entailed in shifting from a primarily agrarian to industrial world. Today, the rapid shift from industrial to postindustrial technologies is still further destabilizing entrenched beliefs and institutions—opening up further opportunities for positive change. But rather than fostering this movement, education is still often hindering it.

The most basic question for our future is what kind of culture is education transmitting. Is it education for a life-enriching culture of partnership and peace? Or is it education for a culture of domination and violence?

As a mother and grandmother, I feel a passionate urgency to help accelerate the global shift toward partnership. I know from both my life and my research that making fundamental changes is not easy. But I also know it can be done. Indeed, it has been done, or we would all still be living in a world where all women and most men knew "their place" in rigid hierarchies of domination. Working together we can create cultures that support rather than inhibit the realization of our highest human potentials: our great capacities for caring, empathy, and creativity. This book—drawing from Marshall Rosenberg's many years of pioneering work in nonviolent, life-enriching, communications—can help us transform education in ways that advance this urgent task.

Riane Eisler

Author of *The Chalice and The Blade, Tomorrow's Children,*
and *The Power of Partnership*

June 25, 2003

Author's Foreword

Public education has for some time been heavily focused on what curricula we believe will be helpful to students. Life-Enriching Education is based on the premise that the relationship between teachers and students, the relationships of students with one another, and the relationships of students to what they are learning are equally important in preparing students for the future.

Children need far more than basic skills in reading, writing, and math, as important as those might be. Children also need to learn how to think for themselves, how to find the meaning in what they learn, and how to work and live together. Teachers, school administrators and parents will come away from Life-Enriching Education with skills in language, communication, and ways of structuring the learning environment that support the development of autonomy and interdependence in the classroom. These skills will help you to prepare students for living in the world they will inherit.

My History in Schools in the United States

I have been consulting with teachers and administrators in public and private schools from the kindergarten to graduate school level for 40 years. During this time I have been helping them integrate this process of education I call Life-Enriching Education into their programs.

I began working with schools while in the private practice of psychology in the early 1960s in St. Louis. Many of the people seeking my services were parents whose children were having problems learning and behaving as school authorities would have liked. Working with the schools in the children's behalf, I began to see that the way schools were structured created suffering for the majority of teachers and students. I saw that the competitiveness fostered in the schools prevented the students from relating in a caring way with one another.

I seldom saw school employees as the problem. In the work I've done over the years in schools, I have been impressed with the vast majority of teachers and administrators with whom I've worked. I have been moved by the care I saw they had for their students and the diligence I saw them demonstrate through their continuing efforts to provide learning opportunities that would enrich their students lives. I saw the teachers and administrators as being brutalized by the educational structures just as much as the students.

My growing awareness of how these educational structures did not support values that were in harmony with my own, led me to explore alternative educational structures. Along with Bill Page, a teacher who had been attending my workshops in Nonviolent Communication I was offering around the city, I explored a different approach to teaching, one in which the teachers relate as partners with the students and the program is designed to promote cooperation instead of competition.

The authorities in Bill's school system were reluctant to agree to his conducting a regular class in this manner, but they did permit him to do it with students who were labeled as disruptive and who were not doing schoolwork anyway. We identified sixty such students; thirty of whom were randomly placed in Bills class and the rest were left in regular classrooms. Academic tests given at the end of the year showed that the students in Bill's class learned far more than those in the traditional classrooms. And when they returned to regular classrooms they had far fewer problems over the next four years than the students who had remained in regular classrooms.

My exploration into alternative approaches was also furthered by the opportunity to work with Tom Shaheen, a visionary superintendent of schools in Rockford, Illinois. He and one of his principals,

JoAnn Anderson, were working to create a school system that fostered respect for diversity, autonomy, and interdependence. I was invited to participate in this venture by contributing to the training of teachers. In the first school developed as part of this project, academic achievement was high, vandalism was significantly reduced, and the program was given a national award for excellence in education.

About this time the War on Poverty was initiated by the Johnson administration. This program provided support for schools in poverty areas to create innovative programs, and I was invited to participate in several of these programs in cities throughout the United States.

Offering Life-Enriching Education Around the World

In the years since, I have regularly continued to assist school systems interested in developing programs supporting respect for diversity and the development of autonomy and interdependence, not only in the United States but in several other countries as well.

Several years ago a principal of a school in Israel, Miri Shapiro, heard of the kinds of school programs I was helping to develop and invited me to support her efforts in creating a similar program in her school. The success of Miri's school led to the European Union financing a program for developing four other schools in Israel and four in the Palestinian Authority. As a result of the success of these additional schools, Miri was appointed as the director of a national commission to prevent violence in the schools. She has now spread the training I offered her to administrators, teachers, parents, and students in more than 400 schools in Israel.

Schools offering Life-Enriching Education, also supported by the European Union, have been established as well in Italy and Serbia.

In the chapters that follow you will find: The opportunity to develop an awareness of the values Life-Enriching Education is designed to support:

- Skills for expressing oneself in ways that supports Life-Enriching Education.

- Skills for empathically connecting with others in ways that supports Life-Enriching Education.

- Means of creating the Life-Enriching partnerships between students, teachers, administrators and parents.

- Means of creating a Life-Enriching learning community in which people contribute to the learning and well-being of each other.

- Means of maintaining Life-Enriching order and safety in schools.

- My dream of Life-Enriching Schools and how to start the transformation.

Marshall Rosenberg

Reigoldswil, Switzerland

. . . let me remind you that information is not knowledge, knowledge is not wisdom, and wisdom is not foresight. Each grows out of the other and we need them all.

—Arthur C. Clarke

CHAPTER 1

Toward Life-Enriching Education

Introduction

I'd like to offer you a vision for the future of education in this country. In this book I will be describing a process of education that can serve, not arbitrary order and authority, but life itself. In this larger dream, we will live in a world in which obedience to authority is no longer a major objective. Before we begin we need to know what our dream is—our ultimate goal. Here is mine—and, I suggest, every human being's dream and goal, at heart: a world nurtured and sustained by Life-Enriching organizations.

I would like to educate this and future generations of children to be able to create new organizations whose goal is to meet human needs—to make life more wonderful for themselves and each other. I call the process of education that can achieve this, *Life-Enriching Education.* I call its opposite *Domination Education.*

Life-Enriching Organizations

Life-Enriching organizations are characterized by fairness and equity in how resources and privileges are distributed. People in positions of leadership *serve* their constituencies rather than desiring to control them. The nature of laws, rules, and regulations are consensually defined, understood, and willingly followed.

Life-Enriching organizations, whether families, schools, businesses, or governments, value the well-being of each person in the community or organization and support Life-Enriching connections between the members of the group.

Life-Enriching human connections have three characteristics:

1) The people are empathically connected to what each is feeling and needing–they do not blame themselves or let judgments implying wrongness obscure this connection to each other.

2) The people are aware of the interdependent nature of their relationships and value the others' needs being fulfilled equally to their own needs being fulfilled–they know that their needs cannot be met at someone else's expense.

3) The people take care of themselves and each other with the sole intention of enriching their lives–they are not motivated by, nor do they use coercion in the form of guilt, shame, duty, obligation, fear of punishment, or hope for extrinsic rewards.

Comparing the Dream to the Nightmare

Perhaps the best way to describe my dream of Life-Enriching organizations is to contrast it with the nightmare of Domination organizations.

DOMINATION ORGANIZATIONS	LIFE-ENRICHING ORGANIZATIONS
Goal:	**Goal:**
Prove who's right, who's wrong	Make life more wonderful
Get what you want	Get everyone's needs met
Obey authority	Connect with self and others

Motivation:	Motivation:
Punishment, reward, guilt, shame, obligation, duty	Contributing to the wellbeing of others Receiving freely from others

Evaluation:	Evaluation:
Labels, judgments	What is fulfilling human needs and what isn't? What would make life more wonderful for you and me?

In a Life-Enriching organization, we get what we want but never at someone else's expense—getting what we want at someone else's expense cannot fulfill all our needs. Our goal in a Life-Enriching organization is far more beautiful—to express our needs without blaming others and to listen respectfully to others' needs, without anyone giving up or giving in—and thus create a quality of connection through which everyone's needs can be met.

Life-Enriching Education

The students coming out of an educational program that I envision would learn to value their autonomy and interdependence, and would have learned the organizational skills necessary to create Life-Enriching systems in which to live their lives.

What you would observe in such schools:

- teachers and students working together as partners, setting objectives mutually and consensually.

- teachers and students speaking a process language. The one I teach is called *Nonviolent Communication*, which focuses attention on: 1) the feelings and needs motivating each person and 2) what actions might best meet their needs—at no one else's expense.

- students motivated by their eagerness to learn and not by fear of punishment or promise of reward.

- tests given at the beginning of the course of study to determine need, not at the end to determine reward or punishment. Grades replaced with evaluations of student learning that describe what they had learned—what skills and knowledge they had mastered.

- an interdependent learning community designed to encourage students to care about one another and help one another learn, rather than competing for a limited number of rewards—a community where the common goal is to support all students in reaching their objectives.

- all rules and regulations being created consensually by the people who are affected by the rules—students, teachers, parents, and administrators. Force only being used to protect needs such as health and safety, but never with the intent to punish.

Changing the System

So what I am advocating is not just a new curriculum, a different daily schedule, an adjustment in classroom arrangement, or some innovative teaching techniques. Many individuals among you have tried the ideas I will suggest in this book, and collectively we have tried all of them. What I am urging is a shift in values, a change in the entire underlying system, something as radical as that.

The people I meet are hungry for such a change, ravenous for it. They realize, along with Morrie Schwartz in Mitch Albom's best-selling *Tuesdays With Morrie*, that "the culture we have does not make people feel good about themselves. We're teaching the wrong things. And you have to be strong enough to say, if the culture doesn't work, don't buy it. Create your own. Most people can't do it."

Maybe alone we can't do it, but the first step in creating a Life-Enriching culture is to be willing to imagine it, and then maybe together, we can.

NVC in Education

Sharing the Field

A Nonviolent Communication (NVC) trainer was teaching NVC to teachers and students at an elementary school. One day while she was there, a conflict occurred on the playground between two groups of boys. It provided an opportunity to demonstrate how NVC skills can be used to mediate conflicts by helping people hear each other's feelings and needs.

It was towards the end of the lunch break and a small group of teachers were on the playground talking with the NVC trainer. Two boys between the ages of 10 and 12 came running up to the NVC trainer. The bigger boy was red in the face and holding tightly on to a ball. The other, smaller, boy was crying.

NVC Trainer (turning, first, to the boy with the ball, and guessing his feelings): You look very excited and upset right now!

Boy 1: Yes. I wanted to play, and because of him *(pointing to the other boy)* I couldn't.

NVC Trainer (hearing his needs and reflecting them): So, you wanted to play and have time with your friends, and this didn't happen?

Boy 1: Yeah, he came and he broke into our game and he wanted to take the ball and we told him many, many times to go away. It's not their time to play now.

NVC Trainer (turning to Boy 2 to see if he was able to hear Boy 1's needs): Can you tell me what you hear him say his needs are?

Boy 2: Yeah, they don't want to play with us.

NVC Trainer (again asking Boy 2): I hear you're frustrated, too, and I would still like to hear from you in your words what do you hear him saying?

Boy 2: That they don't want to be disturbed while they're playing.

NVC Trainer: That's what I hear as well. And now, I'd like to know how that is for you?

Boy 2: We want to play. Just because they're bigger than us, they never give us the field.

NVC Trainer (turning to Boy 1): So, what do you hear him say?

Boy 1: Yeah, they want to play, too, but it's not their time.

NVC Trainer: Hold on. Can you just hear him right now?

Boy 1: Yeah, he wants to play, too.

NVC Trainer: So what I'm hearing is that you both want to play. And you'd both like some say in where and how you can use the field.

Boy 2: But it's not fair. Just because they're bigger, they always get their way.

NVC Trainer (hearing his needs): So you would like respect? And you'd like fairness?

Boy 2: Yeah.

NVC Trainer: I'm guessing you might like to have equal time to play on the field? Would this meet your needs for fairness and for respect?

Boy 2: Yeah.

NVC Trainer (turning to Boy 1): I guess you'd like fairness as well?

Boy 1: Yeah.

NVC Trainer: I'm wondering if you're ready to consider some ways this could happen, or do either of you need more understanding first?

Boy 2: I think he'll just take the field anyway.

Boy 1: How do I know he won't keep butting in?

NVC Trainer: So it sounds to me like you both have a need to trust that the other person will keep whatever agreement you make about dividing up the field?

Boys 1 & 2: Yeah.

NVC Trainer: It seems important, then, that whatever agreement you come up with is one that you both feel comfortable with, and can genuinely say you will try out for a period of time, to see how it works. Would you agree?

Boys 1 & 2 (nodding their heads): Yeah.

NVC Trainer: My guess is that you both have some ideas for how this could get worked out. Would you like to talk by yourselves and then let me or one of your teachers know what ideas you come up with? Or do you want an adult to be with you while you discuss this?

Both boys said they wanted to talk together on their own. After a short while, they came up with a plan to divide the field on some days and take turns using the whole field on other days. They said they would be willing to try this for two weeks and then meet to discuss how it's working.

While the boys were working this out, the NVC trainer turned to the group of teachers who had been watching the mediation.

NVC Trainer: So I'm curious what you observed in this interaction?

Teacher 1: I'm amazed that they worked it out so quickly.

NVC Trainer: So you're amazed, and, I'm guessing, pleased, to see how these students in conflict came to mutual understanding so quickly?

Teacher 1: Yes. And I'm thinking about how I would have handled it and how it probably would have turned out.

NVC Trainer: How is that?

Teacher 1: I probably would have scolded the older boy and told him he couldn't play on the field for a week, or something like that. I'd have punished him in some way. And he would not be talking with the younger boy.

Teacher 2: I was thinking the same thing. Only I probably would have punished the younger boy for breaking into their game. I might have told his whole group to stay off the field for some period of time and think about it until they learn how to get along. But it never works. It just takes the heat off for a while.

NVC Trainer: Hearing this, I imagine you will be interested to see how they are able to continue working things out for themselves?

Teacher 1: Yes. And I'm interested, too, in how I can learn to help them work things out for themselves, like you just did.

CHAPTER 2

Expressing Life-Enriching Messages

Preparing Students

As teachers we can prepare students for participating in and creating Life-Enriching organizations by speaking a language that allows us to truly connect with one another moment by moment. I call this language Nonviolent Communication. By speaking this language we can make partners of teachers and students, give students the tools with which to settle their disputes without fighting, build bridges between former adversaries such as parents and school boards, and contribute to our own well-being and the well-being of others. So, you might ask, why don't we all quickly learn this wonderful language and speak it every day of our lives?

Unfortunately the language we have learned has taught us to judge our own actions and the actions of others in terms of moralistic categories such as "right/wrong," "correct/incorrect," "good/bad," "normal/abnormal," "appropriate/inappropriate."

We have been further educated to believe that persons in positions of authority know which of these judgments best fits any situation. If we find ourselves wearing the label "teacher" or "principal" we think we should know what is best for all those we supervise, and we are quick to label those who do not comply with our decisions as "uncooperative," "disruptive," or even "emotionally disturbed." At the same time, we are calling ourselves "ineffective" if our efforts fail. Our having been educated to use language in this way contributes to the subservience to authority upon which Domination systems depend.

Once I was asked by an interviewer on a radio talk show, "What do you think would create the most peace on earth?" And I said, "If we could teach people to think in terms of their needs rather than in terms of moralistic judgments like right/wrong, good/bad." Whew! You should have seen that switchboard light up! Many people get scared when they hear that, and think that I am recommending making no judgments at all, advocating total permissiveness. On the contrary, people who believe as I believe have strong opinions, powerful values, but they make judgments based on these values instead of moralistic judgments.

So most of us find that Nonviolent Communication is not a difficult language to learn at all. What is difficult is unlearning the language of moralistic judgments, the language of Domination.

The Effects of Moralistic Judgments on Learning

The most powerful way I've been able to get across to teachers the difference between moralistic judgments and value judgments occurred in a school in Norfolk, Virginia. I was showing teachers how they might use value judgments when evaluating students' academic performance. These teachers were skeptical about evaluating a students' work without indicating whether an answer was "right" or "wrong." So I took over several classes including math, science, and language, hoping to convince these teachers that there are alternatives to such judgments. These classes were videotaped.

More than four hours of videotaping was done during that

school day. However, the school authorities later told me that the first ten minutes of videotaping was all that was necessary to convince teachers about the importance of alternatives to moralistic judgments.

During these ten minutes, I came across a nine-year-old boy. He had just finished adding up a page of arithmetic problems, and I saw that he had added up nine plus six to equal fourteen. So I said to him, "Hey buddy, I'm confused about how you got this answer. I get a different one. I'd like you to show me how you got that."

What I said was true. I really was confused how he got that answer. Maybe he'd invented a new system of mathematics I might like better than the one I was taught. Anyway, I was confused whether that was it, or he had done something else. And so I said, "I'm confused how you got this answer. I get a different one. Would you be willing to show me how you got this?"

The boy hung his head and began to cry.

I asked, "Hey, Buddy, what's going on?"

He answered, "I got it wrong."

That's all the teachers needed to see. This child had already learned by the third grade that all that matters in school is how you are evaluated by others. He heard the word "wrong" without my even saying it. Not only did he hear that he was "wrong," but his response communicated how ashamed he was to be "wrong." He probably associated being "wrong" with other painful judgments such as being called "stupid" and with powerful consequences, such as being excluded from some group.

How quickly we contribute to students learning that the most important part of schooling is not the development of Life-Enriching skills and information, but earning positive judgments and avoiding negative ones.

Such learning is critical to maintaining Domination systems in which work is done to gain rewards and avoid punishment. Rewards and punishment are not necessary when people see how their efforts are contributing to their own well-being and the well-being of others.

I recall an elementary school teacher in Texas getting annoyed when I was explaining the benefits of evaluating by using value judgments. She said, "You're making something complicated that doesn't have to be complicated. Facts are facts and I see nothing wrong with a teacher saying a student is right when the student is right and wrong when the student is wrong." I asked the teacher for an example of something that was so factual. She answered, "For example, it is a fact that Christopher Columbus discovered America." That day a Native American friend of mine accompanied me. He calmly said to the teacher, "That isn't what my grandfather told me."

Performance Evaluation Using Value Judgments

Evaluation using value judgments lets the learner know whether or not her performance is or is not in harmony with the needs or values of the instructor. In such evaluation there would be no static, moralistic evaluations usually referred to as "criticism," nor would there be positive evaluations such as "compliments" or "praise." Thus, teachers might evaluate a student's performance by saying, "I agree" or "I disagree," not "That's right" or "That's wrong." Teachers would express what they would like students to do but not use language implying that students had no choice such as, "You have to," or "You can't do that," or "You should," or "You must."

To really get teachers committed to this idea, as difficult as it is, we have a special kind of detector in Life-Enriching Schools. No teacher is allowed through the door who has any of these words in his consciousness: right, wrong, correct, incorrect, good, bad, normal, abnormal, respectful, disrespectful, gifted, not gifted, have to, must, ought, and especially, should.

Students educated in such a judgment-free environment learn because they choose to, not to earn rewards or avoid moralistic judgments or punishment. Every teacher knows, or at least can imagine, the joy of teaching a student who truly wants to learn, an experience that is all too rare.

I hope that by now you are beginning to see that just using a different language to evaluate student performance could radically change our educational systems. And I can also hear you asking, "But what about report cards? What about proficiency and achievement tests?"

I will try to answer those questions. But first I want to describe for you the basics of Nonviolent Communication.

Components of Nonviolent Communication

Nonviolent Communication helps us to be aware of and to clearly express:

- what we are observing that is fulfilling our needs;

- what we are observing that is not fulfilling our needs;

- what we are presently feeling and needing;

- the actions we are requesting to fulfill our needs.

- Opinions and beliefs are expressed as opinions and beliefs and not as facts.

Nonviolent Communication also helps us empathically hear:

- what others are observing that is fulfilling their needs;

- what others are observing that is not fulfilling their needs;

- what others are feeling and needing;

• what actions others are wanting to fulfill their needs.

Remember that our goal and the goal of Nonviolent Communication is not to get what we want, but to make a human connection that will result in everyone getting their needs met. It's as simple, and as complex, as that.

Making Clear Observations Without Mixing in Evaluations

An important part of Nonviolent Communication is the ability to observe what people are doing without mixing in any evaluation that might sound like a criticism. It has been my experience that when people hear criticism, it is unlikely that anyone will get their needs met (for example, the student's need to learn or the teacher's need to teach). Criticism is more likely to provoke defensive arguments or counter-criticism than cooperation.

Even if the person does what we want, he is more likely to be responding out of shame, guilt, or fear of punishment, than out of a desire to fulfill anyone's needs. When people respond for such reasons, it is very costly to all concerned. It is costly to the other person because it is dehumanizing to act out of such intentionality. And it will be costly to us because when we are associated with such dehumanization, it diminishes the other person's enjoyment of contributing to our well-being and even reduce the likelihood that they will want to do so.

Ruth Bebermeyer, composer and poet, wrote the following song to help children learn to observe without evaluating:

> *I've never seen a lazy man;*
> *I've seen a man who never ran*
> *while I watched him, and I've seen*
> *a man who sometimes slept between*

*lunch and dinner, and who'd stay
at home upon a rainy day,
but he was not a lazy man.
Before you call me crazy,
think, was he a lazy man or
did he just do things we label "lazy"?*

*I've never seen a stupid kid;
I've seen a kid who sometimes did
things I didn't understand
or things in ways I hadn't planned;
I've seen a kid who hadn't seen
the same places where I had been,
but he was not a stupid kid.
Before you call him stupid,
think, was he a stupid kid or did he
just know different things than you did?*

*I've looked as hard as I can look
but never ever seen a cook;
I saw a person who combined
ingredients on which we dined,
A person who turned on the heat
and watched the stove that cooked the meat—
I saw those things but not a cook.
Tell me, when you're looking,
Is it a cook you see or is it someone
doing things that we call cooking?*

*What some of us call lazy
some call tired or easy-going,
what some of us call stupid*

some just call a different knowing,
so I've come to the conclusion,
it will save us all confusion
if we don't mix up what we can see
with what is our opinion.
Because you may, I want to say also;
I know that's only my opinion.

What I mean by an observation is something that we can see, hear, or touch, something that could be recorded by a video camera. It is descriptive. An evaluation involves making inferences about the things that we observe. Nonviolent Communication does not suggest that we remain totally objective and refrain from any evaluations. We can tell people how we feel about what we have observed, and what we value. But to shout at a child, "Sharon! That was a mean thing to do, to hit Lionel in the head with a block!" is very different from saying, "I get scared when I see you hitting Lionel with a block, Sharon, because I want everyone to be safe in this classroom!"

The best way I know to demonstrate the difference between observations that are pure observations and those that contain evaluations is a chart such as the following:

Examples of Mixing Observation With Evaluation	Examples of Separating Observation from Evaluation
You are too generous.	When you give all your lunch money to others, I get concerned that you are giving away money that you might need.
Doug procrastinates.	Doug only studies for exams the night before.
He won't get his work in.	He doesn't get his work in.
Minorities don't take care of their property.	I have not seen the minority family living at the house on the corner shovel the snow on their front sidewalk.

Hank Smith is a poor soccer player.	Hank Smith has not scored a goal in 20 games.
Jim is ugly.	I don't find Jim's looks appealing.

Some of the examples in the right hand column contain opinions expressed as opinions, not as facts; others contain no opinions at all, just pure observations.

Exercise 1

Observation or Evaluation?

To determine your proficiency at discerning between observations and evaluations, complete the following exercise. Circle the number in front of any statement that is an observation only, with no evaluation mixed in.

1. "When I asked Maria to please listen to me, she answered back rudely."

2. "Toby told me that the dog ate his homework."

3. "I heard the 6th grader say to the 3rd grader, 'You're stupid.'"

4. "She's very smart."

5. "You're a wonderful writer."

6. "I can't recall a time this week when she arrived at school by the time the bell rang."

7. "He's a bully."

8. "She told me that she has a learning disorder."

9. "I saw her talking and laughing with three other girls, while pointing to the new student."

10. "They were being very disruptive."

Here are my responses for Exercise 1:

1. If you circled this number, we're not in agreement. I consider "rudely" to be an evaluation. An example of an observation without evaluation might be: When I asked Maria to please listen to me, she answered, "I don't have to listen to anybody."

2. If you circled this number, we're in agreement that an observation was expressed without being mixed together with an evaluation.

3. If you circled this number, we're in agreement that an observation was expressed without being mixed together with an evaluation.

4. If you circled this number, we're not in agreement. I consider "very smart" to be an evaluation. An observation without evaluation might be: "She answered every question to my satisfaction on every one of her final exams."

5. If you circled this number, we're not in agreement. I consider "wonderful" to be an evaluation. An observation without evaluation might be, "In your story you used at least three paragraphs to describe the lives of each character."

6. If you circled this number, we're in agreement that an observation was expressed without being mixed together with an evaluation.

7. If you circled this number, we're not in agreement. I consider "bully" to be an evaluation. An observation without evaluation would be, "Six students told me that he threatens them if they don't do what he says,"

or "I have seen him at recess, on several occasions, take the ball out of other students' hands."

8. If you circled this number, we're in agreement that an observation was expressed without being mixed together with an evaluation. While I consider "learning disorder" an evaluation, the statement that "She told me that she has a learning disorder" is an observation of what she did.

9. If you circled this number, we're in agreement that an observation was expressed without being mixed together with an evaluation.

10. If you circled this number, we're not in agreement. I consider "disruptive" an evaluation. An observation without evaluation might be, "they were laughing louder than I would have liked while I was trying to give directions."

Identifying and Expressing Feelings

A basic function of Nonviolent Communication is to focus attention on what we are feeling at any given moment. To do this requires a literacy in the expression of feelings. Unfortunately, having been taught the language of Domination, most of us could come up with ten synonyms for a label such as "stupid," but don't have much in our feelings vocabulary beyond "good" and "bad."

In expressing our feelings, it helps to use words referring to specific emotions in contrast to words that make vague, general statements. If I say, "I feel good about that," or "I feel bad about that," I'm not being very clear about what I am feeling. "Good" could mean elated, encouraged, contentedly at ease, or something in between. "Bad" could be expressing despondency, discouragement, or just mild disappointment.

Our language does not make it easy to convey how we feel. We can actually use the verb "feel" and not be expressing how we feel at all. Note that in the following sentences when the verb feel is followed by the words "that," "like," "as if," "I," "you," "he," "she," or "they," the speaker is not clearly describing a feeling:

- "I feel that you should know better."
- "I feel as if I have better things to do."
- "I feel like I didn't get a fair deal."
- "I feel I am being railroaded."
- "I feel they want me to leave."

We have no idea what the people making the above statements are feeling. We could guess, but we might easily guess wrong. The person making the last statement could be either totally undone or absolutely delighted at the prospect of leaving.

Following is a list of words to help you increase literacy in expressing your feelings. It is by no means exhaustive. Add your own.

Feelings Experienced When Our Needs Are Being Fulfilled

absorbed	encouraged	intrigued	touched
adventurous	energetic	invigorated	tranquil
affectionate	engrossed	involved	trust
alert	enjoyment	joyful	warm
alive	enlivened	jubilant	wide-awake
amazed	enthusiastic	keyed-up	wonderful
amused	exalted	loving	
animated	excited	mellow	
appreciative	exhilarated	merry	
aroused	expansive	mirthful	
astonished	expectant	moved	
blissful	exuberant	optimistic	
breathless	fascinated	overjoyed	
buoyant	free	overwhelmed	
calm	friendly	peaceful	
carefree	fulfilled	pleasure	
cheerful	gay	proud	
comfortable	glad	quiet	
complacent	gleeful	radiant	
composed	glorious	rapturous	
concerned	glowing	refreshed	
confidant	good-humored	relieved	
contented	grateful	satisfied	
cool	gratified	secure	
curious	groovy	sensitive	
dazzled	happy	spellbound	
delighted	helpful	splendid	
eager	hopeful	stimulated	
ecstatic	inquisitive	surprised	
effusive	inspired	tender	
elated	intense	thankful	
electrified	interested	thrilled	

Feelings Experienced When Our Needs Aren't Being Fulfilled

afraid	disgusted	hurt	resentful
aggravated	disheartened	impatient	restless
agitated	disinterested	indifferent	sad
alarm	dislike	inert	scared
aloof	dismayed	infuriated	sensitive
angry	displeased	inquisitive	shaky
anguish	disquieted	insecure	shocked
animosity	distressed	insensitive	skeptical
annoyance	disturbed	intense	sleepy
anxious	downcast	irate	sorrowful
apathetic	downhearted	irked	sorry
apprehensive	dread	irritated	sour
aroused	dull	jealous	spiritless
aversion	edgy	jittery	startled
bad	embarrassed	keyed-up	surprised
beat	embittered	lassitude	suspicious
bitter	exasperated	lazy	tepid
blah	exhausted	let-down	terrified
blue	fatigued	lethargic	thwarted
bored	fear/ful	listless	tired
breathless	fidgety	lonely	troubled
brokenhearted	forlorn	mad	uncomfortable
chagrined	frightened	mean	unconcerned
cold	frustrated	melancholy	uneasy
concerned	furious	miserable	unglued
confused	gloomy	mopey	unhappy
cool	grief	nervous	unnerved
credulous	guilty	nettled	unsteady
cross	hate	overwhelmed	upset
dejected	heavy	passive	uptight
depressed	helpless	perplexed	vexed
despair	hesitant	pessimistic	weary
despondent	horrible	provoked	withdrawn
detached	horrified	puzzled	woeful
disappointed	hostile	rancorous	worried
discouraged	hot	reluctant	wretched
disgruntled	humdrum	repelled	

Exercise 2

Expressing Feelings

If you would like to see whether we're in agreement about the verbal expression of feelings, circle the number in front of any of the following statements in which feelings are verbally expressed.

1. "I feel you are angry."

2. "I'm pleased to see you complete the report."

3. "I feel sad because I'd like everyone to have a sense of belonging at school, and I see that you don't."

4. "You're delightful."

5. "When you showed the new student around, I felt so happy."

6. "I'm grateful that you told me what's troubling you."

7. "I feel like you students aren't trying as hard as you could."

8. "I'm worried that you won't have time to finish that."

9. "When you don't do what I say, I feel disrespected."

10. "I feel happy to see how much you are learning."

Here are my responses for Exercise 2:

1. If you circled this number, we're not in agreement. I don't consider "you are angry" to be a feeling. To me, it expresses what the speaker thinks the other person is feeling, rather than how the speaker is feeling. Whenever the words "I feel" are followed by the words "I," "you," "he," "she," "they," "it," "that," "like," or "as if," what follows is generally not what I would consider to be a feeling. Examples of an expression of feeling might be: "I feel concerned . . . " or "I'm curious . . . "

2. If you circled this number, we're in agreement that a feeling was verbally expressed.

3. If you circled this number, we're in agreement that a feeling was verbally expressed.

4. If you circled this number, we're not in agreement. I don't consider "delightful" to be a feeling. To me, it expresses how the speaker evaluates the other person, as delightful, rather than how the speaker is feeling. An expression of feeling might be: "I feel delighted . . . " or "I feel happy when I see you . . . "

5. If you circled this number, we're in agreement that a feeling was verbally expressed.

6. If you circled this number, we're in agreement that a feeling was verbally expressed.

7. If you circled this number, we are not in agreement. To me, this sentence expresses what the speaker thinks the other person is doing. This is generally the case when the words "I feel" are followed by the word "like." An expression of feeling in this case might be: "I feel sad

and concerned when I see the work you've been turning in."

8. If you circled this number, we're in agreement that a feeling was verbally expressed.

9. If you circled this number, we're not in agreement. I don't consider "disrespected" to be a feeling. To me, it expresses what the speaker thinks the other person is doing. An expression of feeling in this case might be: "I feel disappointed . . . " or "I feel upset . . . "

10. If you circled this number, we're in agreement that a feeling was verbally expressed.

The Risks of Not Expressing Our Feelings

Negative effects can result when we fail to express our feelings. One time I was asked to teach a course in Nonviolent Communication to a group of students in the inner city in St. Louis. When I walked into the room the first day, the students who had been enjoying a lively conversation with one another became silent. When I said, "Good Morning," no one responded. I felt very uncomfortable but was afraid to say so. Instead of expressing my feelings, I continued in my most professional and probably pompous manner saying, "We will be studying a process of communication that I hope you will find helpful in your relationships at home and with your friends." I continued to present information about Nonviolent Communication but no one seemed to be listening. One girl brought out a nail file and started to file her nails. The students near the window looked out to see what was going on in the street below. I felt even more uncomfortable but blundered on.

Finally one of the students with more courage than I was demonstrating, said, "You hate being with black people, don't you?" I immediately realized how covering up my discomfort was contributing to the student's interpretation of what was going on in me.

I replied, "I'm feeling nervous, but not because you're black. My feelings have to do with my not knowing anyone and thinking I was not being accepted when I came in the room."

This expression of my vulnerability had a pronounced effect on the students. They started to ask questions about me, and gradually began telling me some things about themselves and expressing an interest in learning about Nonviolent Communication.

Connecting Our Feelings to our Needs

Nonviolent Communication heightens our awareness that what

others say and do may be the stimulus for our feelings, but are never the cause. Our feelings result from whether our needs are being met or not. So Sharon did not make the teacher feel scared when she hit Lionel in the head with a block; the teacher's fear was caused by his need for the physical safety and well-being of the children in the classroom. If his need at the moment had been for sleep, because he had been up half the night before with a sick child, he might have felt overwhelmed instead of fearful, and simply checked out Lionel's scalp for an open wound and then all but ignored Sharon, because he didn't have the energy to deal with her.

Interpretations, criticisms, diagnoses, and judgments of others are actually alienated expressions of our unmet needs. For example, if a student says to a teacher, "That's not fair! You never pick me!", the student may be expressing her unmet need for equality. Or if a teacher says to a student, "You've been late to class every day this week. You don't care if you learn anything or not, do you?", the teacher may be expressing his unmet need for appreciation for the work that has gone into class preparation and planning.

Expressing our needs in this indirect fashion can be very self-defeating. The more directly we can connect our feelings to our needs the easier it is for others to respond compassionately. On the other hand, when our needs are expressed through interpretations and judgments, people are likely to hear criticism. And, as I said before, when people hear anything that sounds like criticism, their energy is more invested in defensiveness and counter criticism than in responding compassionately.

However, most of us have not been taught to think in terms of our needs. Rather we have been educated to think in terms of what is wrong with others when our needs are not being fulfilled. Thus we may interpret our students as "lazy" for not completing work on time or "irresponsible" for leaving their homework at home. Over and over again, it has been my experience that from the moment people begin talking about what they are needing rather than what's wrong with the other person, the possibility of finding ways to meet everyone's needs is greatly increased.

The following are some of the basic needs we all share:

Autonomy
  to choose one's dreams/goals/values
  to choose one's plan for fulfilling one's dreams/goals/values

Celebration
  celebrate the creation of life
  celebrate losses: loved ones, dreams, etc. (mourning)

Integrity
  authenticity
  meaning
  creativity

Interdependence
  acceptance
  appreciation
  closeness
  consideration
  contribute to the enrichment of life (exercise one's power to contribute to the well-being of others and one's own well-being)
  emotional safety
  empathy
  honesty
  empowering honesty (that which enables us to learn from our limitations)

  love
  reassurance
  respect
  support
  trust
  warmth

Physical nurturance
  air
  food, water
  movement/exercise
  protection from life-threatening forms of life: viruses, bacteria, insects, and predatory animals
  rest
  sexual expression
  shelter
  touch

Play
  fun, pleasure, self-expression

Spiritual communion
  beauty
  harmony
  inspiration
  order
  peace

I consider the above list a work in progress and always welcome changes and additions to it. A teacher friend of mine made up her own list of needs, which she found to be helpful in working with young people:

What Do You Need?

autonomy, to make choices; accomplishment; affection; appreciation; beauty; chances to help others; creative expression; dignity; exercise; food, water, air, warmth; fun and play; harmony; honesty, truthfulness; learning new skills; love and belonging; order; peace; reassurance; respect; rest; safety, security; space; support; touch; trust; understanding

Have fun making up your own list. Just be sure you include only universal human needs.

Exercise 3

Acknowledging Needs

To practice identifying needs, please circle the number in front of any statement whereby the speaker is acknowledging responsibility for his or her feelings by showing how their feelings are connected to their needs.

1. "I feel relieved that you returned when you did because I was concerned for your safety."

2. "I feel upset hearing you call her a name because I need respect for everyone."

3. "I'm excited about your report."

4. "I'm hurt when you say, 'I don't care.'"

5. "When you come late to class I feel frustrated."

6. "It makes me mad when you scribble on your paper."

7. "I'm disappointed because I wanted to get my point across clearly, and I see that I didn't."

8. "You make me so happy when you help each other."

9. "I'm puzzled when you do things like that."

10. "I'm grateful that you spoke up because I value honesty."

Here are my responses for Exercise 3:

1. If you circled this number, we're in agreement that the speaker is acknowledging responsibility for his or her feelings.

2. If you circled this number, we're in agreement that the speaker is acknowledging responsibility for his or her feelings.

3. If you circled this number, we're not in agreement. To express the needs or thoughts underlying his or her feelings, the speaker might have said, "I'm excited about your report because I've been wanting to learn more about dolphins."

4. If you circled this number, we're not in agreement. To me, the statement implies that the other person's behavior is solely responsible for the speaker's feelings. It doesn't reveal the speaker's needs or thoughts that are contributing to his or her feelings. To do so, the speaker might have said, "When you say 'I don't care,' I feel hurt, because my need for consideration is not met."

5. If you circled this number, we're not in agreement. To express the needs and thoughts underlying his or her feelings, the speaker might have said, "When you come late to class I feel frustrated because I have a need to use our time in a way that contributes to everyone's learning."

6. If you circled this number, we're not in agreement. To express the needs and thoughts underlying his or her feelings, the speaker might have said, "When you scribble on your paper, I feel angry because I have a need to conserve our resources"

7. If you circled this number, we're in agreement that the speaker is acknowledging responsibility for his or her feelings.

8. If you circled this number, we're not in agreement. To express the needs and thoughts underlying his or her feelings, the speaker might have said, "I'm happy when I see you helping each other because I value cooperation and shared learning."

9. If you circled this number, we're not in agreement. To express the needs and thoughts underlying his or her feelings, the speaker might have said, "I'm puzzled when you do things like that. I'd like to understand what need you're trying to meet."

10. If you circled this number, we're in agreement that the speaker is acknowledging responsibility for his or her feelings.

Requesting That Which Would Make Life More Wonderful

So suppose a student comes to your English class for the fifth time this week without having done his homework assignment, and since you have decided to use Nonviolent Communication with your students, you bite back the impulse to call him lazy and irresponsible. Instead you tell him what you are observing without mixing in any evaluation, ("When you answer my question by saying you didn't read the assignment"), tell him how you feel about this ("I feel puzzled"), and connect that feeling to your need ("because I need to contribute to my students' learning, and I can't see how you can learn about American literature without reading some of it"). So far so good.

The final step is to clearly convey to your student what he could do to meet your needs. This can sometimes be the most difficult step. You have already asked him five times, to read specific pages in Huckleberry Finn and he hasn't done it, so there's no point in asking him again. What can you suggest of him that can make a connection with him, and eventually result in both of your needs being met?

To find the answer to that question, let's start by considering what requests sound like using Nonviolent Communication. First of all, Nonviolent Communication involves expressing what we are requesting rather than what we are not requesting. Confusion often results when we are told what not to do. My favorite example is the preschooler who was told to stop pinching her classmates when she felt annoyed with them. So the next time a child took a toy she wanted, she bit him.

In addition to making our requests in terms of what we do want, we make our requests in terms of concrete actions, avoiding vague, abstract language. When we express requests in clear action language we increase the likelihood that others will be more willing to respond to them.

The confusion that can be caused by vague or ambiguous language when making requests was amusingly demonstrated by a cartoon showing a man who has fallen into a lake and can't swim. He shouts to his dog on shore, "Lassie, get help!" In the next picture you see the dog on a psychiatrist's couch.

One time I was invited to work with some high school students who had several grievances with their school principal whom they interpreted as a racist. A minister, who was working closely with this group of students, was aware that they were planning some violent retaliation against the principal. Very concerned about this, he asked the students to first meet with me. Out of respect for the minister, they agreed.

At our meeting, the students began by expressing that they believed they were being unfairly discriminated against. After hearing several comments, I suggested that they clarify what they would like to request from the principal.

One of the students responded disgustedly, "What good would that do? We already went to the principal and told him what we wanted and he said, 'Get out of here! I don't need you people telling me what to do.'"

I asked the students what they had requested at that meeting. They told me how they had first told the principal that they did not want him telling them how to wear their hair. I shared with the students that I thought they might have received a more cooperative response if they had expressed what they did want, rather than what they did not want.

They next related to me that they had told the principal that they wanted to be treated more fairly. Again, I shared with the students that I believed they were more likely to have received a cooperative response if they had described the specific actions that they were requesting, rather than to use a vague term such as "fair treatment."

We worked together to find ways they could express their requests in positive action language. At the end of our meeting, the students had clarified 38 actions that they wanted to happen at their school.

The day following our meeting, the students went in, once again, and expressed their requests to the principal—only this time, they expressed their requests using the clear action language we had practiced. Later that night, they called, elated, and told me that the principal had agreed to all 38 of their requests. Three days later, a representative from the school district called me to inquire about my coming to district to teach their administrators what I had taught the students.

The Difference Between Requests and Demands

A third aspect of making requests in Nonviolent Communication involves knowing the difference between requests and demands. When others hear our requests as demands, they believe that if they do not say "yes," they will be blamed or punished. Once they hear a request as a demand they see only the options of submission or rebellion. Either way, they experience us as coercive, and they are not likely to respond compassionately to what we have requested.

For example, if a teacher says to a student, "Would you be willing to move your seat to the back of the room so that I can put my fossil table here?" that could be either a request or a demand, as I'm defining those terms. The difference between a request and a demand is not determined by how politely we speak. The difference is seen by how the person making the request treats others when they do not comply with the request.

So if the student responds to the teacher's request by saying, "I'd rather stay where I am," and the teacher then says, "That's not very considerate of you!" then I would call it a demand. The teacher has moralistically judged the student's preference rather than wanting to understand the student's motivation.

Here is a similar scenario:

Teacher: Would you be willing to move your seat to the back of the room so that I can put my fossil table here?

Student: I'd rather keep my seat where it is.

Teacher: You hurt my feelings when you refuse to do what I ask you to. You know how much my fossil collection means to me.

In this scenario we see that when the student says "no," the teacher implies that the student has hurt her feelings. When we blame others for our feelings, we are often hoping that they will feel guilty when they don't do as we have asked. The more we take a "no" as rejection or as the cause of our unhappiness, the more our requests are likely to be heard in the future as demands.

Exercise 4

Expressing Requests

To see whether we're in agreement about the clear expression of requests, circle the number in front of any of the following statements in which the speaker is clearly requesting that a specific action be taken.

1. "I want you to be respectful."

2. "I'd like you to pay attention when I'm talking."

3. "I'd like you to tell me what your understanding is of my objectives for this project."

4. "I would like you to be on time in the future."

5. "I'd like you to tell me if you'd be willing to schedule a time to talk about what happened with you and Toby today."

6. "I'd like you to try harder."

7. "I'd like you to put away all the materials you've been working with in the next five minutes."

8. "I'd like you to use your words to tell her what's going on."

9. "I'd like you to raise your hand at any point that you don't understand my directions. Is anyone unwilling to do this?"

10. "I'd like us to play fair."

Here are my responses for Exercise 4:

1. If you circled this number, we're not in agreement. To me, the words "be respectful" do not clearly express a specific action that is being requested. The speaker might have said, "I'd like you to answer my question or tell me what need of yours prevents you from doing so."

2. If you circled this number, we're not in agreement. To me, the words "pay attention" do not clearly express a specific action that is being requested. The speaker might have said, "after I finish what I'm about to say, I'd like you to tell me back what you heard me say"

3. If you circled this number, we're in agreement that the statement clearly expresses what the speaker is requesting.

4. If you circled this number, we're not in agreement. To me, the words "be on time" do not clearly express a specific action being requested. The speaker might have said, "I would like you to tell me if you would be willing from now on to have your jackets and backpacks put away and be sitting at your desks by the time the bell rings?"

5. If you circled this number, we're in agreement that the statement clearly expresses what the speaker is requesting.

6. If you circled this number, we're not in agreement. To me, the words "try harder" do not clearly express a specific action being requested. The speaker might have said, "I'd like you to tell me what I could do to support you focusing on this work until it is completed."

7. If you circled this number, we're in agreement that the statement clearly expresses what the speaker is requesting.

8. If you circled this number, we're not in agreement. The words "use your words" do not clearly express a specific action being requested. The speaker might have said, "I'd like you to tell her what she did that you didn't like, how you feel, and what need of yours was not met."

9. If you circled this number, we're in agreement that the statement clearly expresses what the speaker is requesting.

10. If you circled this number, we're not in agreement. The words "play fair" do not clearly express a specific action being requested. The speaker might have said, "I'd like you to tell me if you would be willing to have each person take only one turn until everyone has had a turn."

The Process is the Objective

If our objective is simply to change people's behavior or to get what we want, Nonviolent Communication is not the language for us. This is a language for those of us who want people to say "yes" to our requests only if they can do so willingly and compassionately.

Since the objective of Nonviolent Communication is to create the quality of connection necessary for everyone's needs to get met, when we speak it we are not simply trying to get people to do what we want. And when people learn to trust that our commitment is to the quality of the relationship—to honesty and empathy—and that our goal is for everyone's needs to be fulfilled, they can trust that our requests are requests and not demands.

So the teacher who wanted to rearrange the classroom might have discovered, through her willingness to understand her student's preference not to move her desk, that the student was having vision problems and wanted to keep her seat where it was, near the front of the room. In the course of that conversation, another student might have volunteered to move his desk to make room for the fossil table. Thus everyone's needs would have been met, and no one would have been criticized or guilt-tripped.

My own children gave me some powerful lessons about demands. Somehow I got it into my head that as a parent it was my job to make demands. My children taught me that I could make all the demands in the world and I still couldn't make them do anything.

That's a humbling lesson in power when you think that because you're the parent, or the teacher, or the school superintendent, that it's your job to change other people and make them behave. But here were my children educating me that I couldn't make them do anything. All I could do was to make them wish they had. And they taught me that any time I would be foolish enough to do that, they would make me wish that I hadn't made them wish they had.

People Can Hear Demands
No Matter What We Say

Some people, of course, will hear demands and criticism no matter how hard we try to avoid these forms of communication. We are particularly likely to be interpreted as expressing demands when we are in a position of authority and the people we are speaking with have had experiences in the past with people who have exercised their authority in a coercive way.

For example, the school administration in a high school asked me to demonstrate for the teachers how Nonviolent Communication could be applied when communicating with students who weren't cooperating as the teachers would have liked. It was arranged for me to meet with forty students labeled by the faculty and administration as "socially and emotionally maladjusted."

It has been my experience that when we give people such labels we are likely to act toward them in a way that contributes to the very behavior that concerns us. Then we use the behavior as confirmation that our diagnosis is accurate. If you were a student and knew you were labeled "socially and emotionally maladjusted" wouldn't that contribute to your resisting whatever was asked of you? Therefore, I wasn't surprised that when I walked into that classroom about half of the students were hanging out the window hollering obscenities at their friends in the courtyard down below.

I started by making a request saying, "I would like you all to come over and sit down so I can tell you who I am, and what I would like us to do today." About half the students came over. I wasn't certain that all the students heard me so I repeated my request. The remainder of the students gradually returned to their seats with the exception of two young men who still stood over by the window. Unfortunately for me, those two were the largest students in the class.

EXPRESSING LIFE-ENRICHING MESSAGES

Addressing the two, I said, "Excuse me, would one of you gentlemen tell me what you heard me say?" One looked at me menacingly and snorted, "Yeah. You said we had to come over there and sit down." I thought to myself, "Uh, oh! He's heard my request as a demand."

I then said to him, "Sir, . . . " (I have learned to always say "Sir" when people have biceps like he did—especially when there's a tattoo on the biceps) "would you be willing to tell me how I could have let you know what I was wanting so that it wouldn't sound like I was saying you had to do it??" He said, "Huh?" Having been conditioned to hear demands coming from authorities, it obviously was not easy for him to hear my request as a request and not as a demand.

So I tried to express this in another way, asking, "How can I let you know what I'm wanting from you so it doesn't sound like I'm bossing you around?"

He thought for a moment about what I said and replied, "I don't know."

I then said, "What is going on between you and me right now is a good example of what I was wanting us to talk about today. I believe people can enjoy each other a lot better if they can say what they would like without bossing others around. However, I don't know what to say so that you will trust that when I tell you what I would like, I am not saying that you have to do it and that I'll try to make your life miserable if you don't." To my relief he seemed to understand what I was saying. He and his friend joined the group and we had a very productive day.

We can help others trust that our request is a request and not a demand by adding some words indicating that we would want people to do what we are asking only if they can do so willingly. Thus we might say, "Would you be willing to wash the chalkboard?" rather than, "I would like you to wash the chalkboard." However, the most powerful way we communicate that our requests are not demands is by empathizing with people when they do not comply with our requests.

So back to the student who wouldn't read Huckleberry Finn. You have told him that you feel puzzled (you also feel discouraged, but the more neutral "puzzled" is less likely to be interpreted as guilt-tripping) and that you need to contribute to his learning but can't figure out how he can learn without reading the book. So now you come up with your request: it is positive, it is concrete, it is immediate, and it is a request instead of a demand: "Would you be willing to tell me what keeps you from reading Huckleberry Finn?"

By now we have covered the first half of the Nonviolent Communication model, the half about speaking this Life-Enriching language. The other half comes next, the half about listening with Life-Enriching ears, so that you will know what to say when your student answers, "Huckleberry Finn is boring."

NVC in Education

Fun For Everyone

A teacher was teaching Nonviolent Communication to a group of 15 children, ages 5-8, in an After School Program. The group met in the school gym every day after school. For the first twenty minutes they ate a snack and talked and played with each other. Then the teacher introduced an activity or game that she hoped would provide a fun way to learn NVC skills.

One day they were playing a cooperative game where each person puts a beanbag on their head, and while music plays, they walk or run around the gym trying to keep the beanbag on their head. If the beanbag falls off, they have to freeze. They can't pick up their own beanbag, but must wait for someone else to pick it up and put it on their head, at which time they can move again. After playing this way for a time, two boys started knocking bean bags off of other kids' heads and pretty soon, all of the kids were racing around knocking beanbags off of each other's heads.

The teacher was very frustrated and anxious. She wanted order and wanted to make sure that everyone was safe. She shouted, "I want everyone to sit down on the floor in a circle right now!"

About half of the kids ran to the circle painted on the floor and sat down, while the others kept running around, gathering speed, as they started throwing bean bags at each other.

"Stop right now!" *she shouted, even louder than before.* "I want you to come sit down right now."

While the students made their way to the circle, a 7-year-old boy named Sean walked up to the teacher and the following dialogue ensued:

Sean: Ms. Mary, you're feeling angry, aren't you?

Teacher (surprised and grateful to be heard): Wow. Yes, Sean, I am feeling pretty frustrated right now. I feel heart-warmed that you noticed. I'm curious. How did you know what I was feeling?

Sean: I could tell by the way you were snatching the beanbags off the floor.

Teacher (laughing): So you could see pretty clearly that I was upset?

Sean: Yeah.

Teacher: Well, it sure helps me to have you see that. I'm feeling more relaxed already.

The teacher then asked everyone to please be quiet.

Teacher (addressing all the students now seated on the circle): A few minutes ago when I yelled at you to stop and come sit down, I was feeling pretty frustrated. I want us to play and learn together. I want it to be fun and what was happening wasn't fun for me, mostly because I was worried someone would get hurt. Would someone tell me what you're hearing me say so far?

Student 1: You said you thought we'd hurt each other.

Student 2: And you said you were frustrated.

Teacher: Thank you for hearing that. It feels so good to be heard. I'm grateful too, that Sean came up to me and asked if I was angry. I was pretty upset for a few minutes. I'm feeling more relaxed now, but I'd still like to see how we can have more fun together in a way that I'm not worried about safety. I'd like to hear from you how you experienced that game.

Student 3: I thought it was fun. I wanted to play longer.

Student 4: Yeah, nobody was getting hurt.

Student 5: It hurt me when you hit my head.

Student 4: No it didn't.

Teacher: So it sounds like some people were having fun and some were not having fun. Is that accurate?

They nod their heads.

Teacher: I'd like to find a way to play where everyone is having fun and everyone is safe. Does anyone have an idea about how this could happen?

The teacher and students spent the rest of the time discussing ways that everyone could have fun. As so often happens, this real life exercise in finding a way that was fun for everyone turned out to provide more valuable learning for the group than the games the teacher had planned for that day. They ended the session by deciding to try three different versions of the game the next time they met to see which would best meet all of their needs.

CHAPTER 3

Hearing Messages With Empathy

Empathy

In this chapter I will discuss ways of empathically hearing messages being expressed by others, listening with Life-Enriching ears. Empathy is a special kind of understanding not to be confused with intellectual understanding, or even with sympathy. Empathy requires listening with the whole being, the hearing that the philosopher Chuang-Tzu refers to in the following passage:

> *The hearing that is only in the ears is one thing. The hearing of the understanding is another. But the hearing of the spirit is not limited to any one faculty, to the ear, or to the mind. Hence it demands the emptiness of all the faculties. And when the faculties are empty, then the whole being listens. There is then a direct grasp of what is right there before you that can never be heard with the ear or understood with the mind.*
> —Thomas Moore's book on the work of Chuang-Tzu

One component of empathy is to be fully present to what the other person is currently feeling and needing, and not losing that through a fog of diagnosis or interpretation. This requires that our minds not wander off on paths of analysis while we seem to be listening to the person before us. We don't want to be like the man in the cartoon who, when his friend says, "I get the feeling you are not listening when I talk to you," answers, "You're right. I'd rather be listening to what I'm going to say next than to what you are saying now."

This being fully present also requires that we clear our consciousness of whatever preconceived ideas or judgments we may have been harboring about the person speaking. I would not want this to sound like I am advocating suppressing or repressing one's feelings. It is more a matter of being so focused on the feelings of the speaker that our own reactions do not intrude.

I find the following analogy helpful in making clear the nature of the focus that empathy requires. Recall a time when you had a pain in your body, perhaps a headache or a toothache, and you became totally engrossed in a book. What happened to the pain? You no longer felt it. You didn't suppress it; rather the focus of your attention was so fully on what you were reading that you were not aware of the pain. In empathy our attention is so fully focused on the feelings and needs of the other person at that moment that we are not aware of our thoughts about the person.

This analogy of the pain in our body can also help us to clarify the difference between empathy and sympathy. At the moment we say to someone, "I feel sad to hear you are in such pain," we are not empathically connecting with the other person's pain. We are expressing the pain we feel that was stimulated by the other's pain. That is sympathy. A sympathetic response can also be a gift to the other person if our timing is right. If we respond sympathetically after we have connected empathically, this can deepen our connection with the other person. However, if we respond with sympathy when the other person needs empathy, this can disconnect us.

Verbally Reflecting What We Hear

Listening intently is one part of empathy. Another is making sure that we heard what we thought we heard. "I know you believe you understood what you think I said, but I am not sure you realize that what you heard is not what I meant." A teacher in a workshop I conducted gave this quote of unknown origin to me. I liked how clearly it alerts us to the fact that we may be convinced that we know exactly what the other person meant, even when we do not. Putting into words our understanding of the speaker's feelings and needs is a way we can verify whether or not we fully understand.

So we might respond to a kindergartener who wails, "I want to go home!" with, "Are you missing your mom, and wishing that you were at home with her?" only to hear back, "No! I found a bird's nest yesterday and I want to go home and get it and show it to everybody."

There are two reasons why we might choose to do this verbal reflection. The first is to make sure that we are accurately understanding what the other person is feeling and needing. By verbally reflecting, others can correct us if our understanding is not what they have been trying to express.

A second reason for verbally reflecting our understanding would be because we sense that the speaker would appreciate some confirmation that she has been understood. When we verbally express empathy is this way, we want to guess what the other person is feeling and needing, rather than tell her what she feels and needs. If we are mistaken, we let her correct us. We do not want to imply that we know better what is going on inside her than she does.

This would be true even if the person to whom we would like to offer empathy has said nothing at all. Thus, one might ask a child standing alone on the edge of the playground, "Are you feeling lonely because you want friends to play with, and the other kids aren't playing with you?" And not, as if stating a fact, "I see that you are feeling lonely because you want friends to play with."

Sometimes our empathy can be communicated nonverbally and no verbal reflection is necessary. When we are fully present to what is alive in others, we wear a different expression than when we are mentally analyzing the person or thinking of what we are going to say next. However empathy is expressed, it touches a very deep need in human beings to feel that someone else can truly hear them, and hear them nonjudgmentally.

When we have connected empathically with the feelings and needs being expressed by the people speaking with us, we then try to clarify what the speakers might want of us. Sometimes speakers may be ready to move quickly to their requests. However, the first feelings and needs they have expressed may be connected to other feelings and needs, and they may need more empathy before moving to their requests. (The lonely child may also be feeling scared or angry, for example, because he had previously had a disagreement with one of his classmates.)

Two signs indicate that speakers may be ready to move to their requests. First, when people have had the empathy they need at a given time, they feel relieved, and we can usually sense this relief. Another more obvious sign is that they stop talking. However, it doesn't hurt to ask them, "Is there more you would like to say?" before moving to their requests.

Listening for Requests

What might people's requests be after feeling our empathy? Sometimes they will be hungry to know how we feel about what they have told us. Sometimes they would appreciate knowing whether we would be willing to take certain actions to fulfill the needs they have been expressing. One way to get this information is to sense what they are requesting and check out whether our guess is accurate. Thus, we might say to the lonely child, "Would you like me to help you find someone to play with?"

If we are not able to sense what the feelings, needs, or requests of others are, we can, of course, ask that the speakers tell us. (We might ask the solitary child, for example, "Is something wrong? Do you want to tell me about it?"). However, others often do not have the literacy to clearly express their feelings, needs, and requests. For this reason I have found it more helpful, whenever possible, to sense the feelings and needs being expressed and check out whether I have guessed accurately.

Connecting Empathically

To help teachers develop their ability to connect empathically with students, I often play the role of a student who has not completed assigned work and who states when questioned about it, "I hate doing this work; it's boring. I want to do something else." At this point, the teacher I'm working with might say, "It's silly to offer empathy for that; it's obvious what the student is feeling and needing." I then ask the teacher to check it out with me by empathizing with what I (in the student's role) have said. So the teacher tries to empathize, "So are you saying you don't want to do anything that requires a little work." At this point, I indicate that such a response is an intellectual interpretation of the student's feelings and needs, but not an attempt to connect with the student's feelings and needs

So we try again. I repeat (in the student's role), "I hate doing this work; it's boring and I want to do something else."

The teacher then might state, "Oh, so you're saying you want me to let you do whatever you want today." I point out that the teacher is mixing up what might be the student's request with the student's needs. I remind the teacher that needs contain no reference to specific people taking specific actions.

It is not rare to find that it takes four or five attempts on the part of a teacher to accurately reflect what might be the student's feelings and needs.

Following are some common reactions on the part of teachers in response to the message, "I hate doing this work. It's boring. I want to do something else."

Justifying or explaining: "This work is very important if you want to go to college."

Probing (questions that try to get at information other than the person's feelings and needs): "What's boring about it?"

Claiming understanding but not checking out understanding: "I understand." or "I used to feel that way too."

Apologizing or sympathizing: "I'm sorry you feel that way." Or "I'm sad that you feel that way."

Judging: "That's foolish. Huckleberry Finn is a classic."

Agreeing: "I agree with you. I never liked that book either."

Disagreeing: "I disagree with you; Huckleberry Finn is my favorite book."

Interpreting: "You are just trying to get out of work."

Advising: "Why don't you wait a few minutes and see if you feel differently."

Personalizing: "I must be a terrible teacher if I can't make Huckleberry Finn interesting."

Going directly to problem solving: "What could we do to make it more interesting?"

Finally, the teacher will say, "So you get bored when you read Huckleberry Finn, and get tired trying to plow through it?"

"Yeah, it's not even in good English."

"You really get bored and tired when you get to the parts in dialect?"

"Yeah, I can't even understand it."

"So are you feeling frustrated, and needing some help?"

A frequently raised concern about empathy is "Wouldn't the student think that you are condoning his thoughts and feelings if you reflect them back that way?" In response I try to make it clear that there is a difference between empathic understanding and agreement. I can show understanding of a student's feelings and needs without implying that I agree, condone, or even like his feelings and needs.

Another concern that I have heard teachers raise is that offering empathy means a commitment to long, drawn out discussions that are not practical, given the time pressures that often exist in the classroom. Teachers often ask me, "What are all the other students in the classroom doing while I take all this time giving empathy to one student?" I believe empathy can often be a timesaving process rather than a time-consuming one.

I am aware of studies that have been done in labor management negotiations indicating that the time needed to settle disputes can be considerably shortened if one simple rule is followed: each participant must paraphrase what the previous speaker has said before saying anything in rebuttal.

I find the same process happening in a classroom. Once the student sees that the teacher wants to understand rather than coerce, a cooperative attitude is more likely to develop that hastens rather than impedes problem solving. So when teachers say to me, "But in the classroom you have to tell children what to do; you can't be spending all of your time showing them that you understand," I remind them that they spend a considerable portion of their day telling students what to do over and over again. By the time a teacher has told a student several times to do something and the student continues not to do it, the time spent is often more than if the teacher had taken time to fully understand the student's feelings and needs at the outset.

I have often found teachers confusing empathizing with parroting or simply mirroring back the exact words of the speaker. I define the process of empathy as similar to the process of translating a foreign language into one's own language. In translating, the goal is to get at the exact meaning of the original message and then translate it into more familiar terms. Likewise, in offering empathy the goal is to translate the message being expressed into feelings and needs.

Some or many of the words reflected back might be the exact ones the speaker is using if she is expressing feelings and needs. Of course, our intent is even more important than what words we use. Our intent is to empathically connect with the other person. Sometimes our look, or a touch, communicates the empathic connection without our having to say anything at all.

A friend of mine, the principal of a school we were transforming into a school based on the principles of Nonviolent Communication, shared the following story with me.

"I came back from lunch one day and found Mildred (an elementary school student) sitting dejectedly on a chair waiting for me. I sat down on a chair next to her and she began, 'Mrs. Anderson, have you ever had a week when everything you did hurt somebody else, and you never intended to hurt anyone at all?'

'Yes,' I answered, 'I think I understand.'

Mildred then went on to tell me a little about what had happened that week with her sister and in her class with the kids and teacher. Now, I was late for a very important meeting, still had my coat on, and was anxious not to keep a room full of people in the meeting waiting, and so I asked, 'Mildred, what can I do for you?'

Mildred moved in her chair so that she took both of my shoulders in her hands, looked me straight in the eyes and said very firmly, 'Mrs. Anderson, I don't want you to do anything; I just want you to listen.'

This was one of the most significant learning experiences in my life—taught to me by a child. I decided, 'The hell with the room of adults.' Mildred and I moved over to a bench which gave us privacy and we sat with my arm around her shoulders and her head on my chest, with her arm around my waist while she talked until she was through."

Empathically Connecting With Others When They Don't Know How to Express Themselves or Choose Not To

Unfortunately I do not find many students who are willing to share their feelings and needs the way Mildred did. They have also been taught the language of Domination systems so they have learned to disguise their messages in various ways. Therefore I like teachers to be able to get in touch with the student's feelings and needs even when the student does not know how to openly express them.

To learn to empathize when others are not directly expressing feelings and needs, I remind myself that what I might be interpreting as attack, criticism, or insult, could be better understood as the speaker having needs that are not being met and his being in pain about this. Or as Hugh Prather expressed this idea, "If someone criticizes me, I am not any less because of that. It is not criticism of me, but critical thinking from him. He is expressing his thoughts and feelings, not my being." (Notes to Myself, Hugh Prather 1970)

In order to empathize when the student isn't openly sharing himself the teacher needs to learn to find the feelings and reasons for the feelings in the following types of messages: demands, judgments, questions, nonverbal messages, and requests.

The following are some examples of a teacher offering empathy for an unexpressed feeling or need:

Situation #1: Teacher expresses frustration in relation to a student behaving in a certain way.

> *Student message:* "You're mean!"

> *Teacher's empathy:* "Are you feeling hurt and needing more respect than you heard in the way I just spoke to you?"

Situation #2: Student comes into class in the morning, doesn't speak with anyone, and sits off by herself.

> *Student message: Student is silent and has a look on her face that teacher interprets as expressing pain.*

> *Teacher's empathy:* "Are you feeling upset and needing some understanding?

Situation #3: Other students have told a student to leave them alone.

> *Student's message:* "No one likes me."

> *Teacher's empathy:* "Are you feeling sad and needing acceptance from the others?"

Situation #4: Parent has asked for a meeting with the teacher to talk about problems his daughter has been having with the teacher.

> *Parent's message:* "My daughter got along with all her other teachers just fine."

Teacher's empathy: "Are you feeling annoyed, and needing assurance that your daughter is getting the attention she needs?"

I was working with a group of 8th graders in a school in Washington and was teaching them to connect with the feelings and needs behind any message. I asked them to identify a list of things their parents, teachers, and classmates were saying that they were interpreting as criticism, and demonstrated how they could learn to sense what the feelings and needs were behind these statements. I told them that each message that sounded like criticism was really a song that I would sing for them. The song was "See Me Beautiful," by Kathy and Red Grammer.

See Me Beautiful
Look for the best in me.
That's what I really am
And all I want to be.
It may take some time,
It may be hard to find,
But see me beautiful.

See me beautiful
Each and every day:
Could you take a chance,
Could you find a way
To see me shining through
In everything I do
And see me beautiful?

(See Me Beautiful by Kathy & Red Grammer
© 1986 Smilin Atcha Music Inc. Available from
Red Note Records 800-824-2980)

A month later I was back in the same city and was talking to a teacher from the school. The teacher said to me, grinning, "Are you aware of what monsters you created? Every time we start to yell at the children now they put their arms around one another and sing, "See me beautiful!"

Exercise 5

Differentiating Between Receiving Empathically And Non-Empathically

If you would like an exercise to see whether we are in agreement about empathy, please circle the number in front of the statements in which person B is responding empathically to what is going on within Person A.

1. *Person A (student):* Nobody likes me.

   Person B (teacher): Yes they do. They just don't know you very well because you're shy.

2. *Person A (student):* I can't do these math problems. I'm stupid.

   Person B (teacher): Do you feel frustrated and want to understand math better?

3. *Person A (parent):* My daughter won't talk to me about anything.

   Person B (teacher): Have you tried listening more?

4. *Person A (school principal):* You need to bring your students' test scores up.

   Person B (teacher): Are you worried and want to protect us from any unpleasant consequences that might happen if we don't show higher test scores?

5. *Person A (student):* Pat's always the teacher's pet.

   Person B (teacher): Are you mad because I ask her to help me a lot?

6. *Person A (student):* I hate school.

   Person B (teacher): I know just how you feel. I didn't

like school when I was your age.

7. *Person A (student):* I think it's unfair that the other class gets a longer recess longer than we do.

   Person B (teacher): That's because they're younger.

8. *Person A (parent):* You give your students too much homework. My daughter is in tears every night trying to get it done.

   Person B (teacher): Are you feeling concerned about your daughter's health and well-being?

9. *Person A (student):* I don't want to talk about it.

   Person B (teacher): I don't see how we're going to work this out if you won't talk about it.

10. *Person A (student):* I don't want the bell to ring. I'll never get to finish my story.

    Person B (teacher): Are you feeling frustrated because you really want to complete your story now that you're so close?

Here are my responses for Exercise 5:

1. I didn't circle this one because I hear Person B giving reassurance and then offering an analysis instead of empathically receiving what is going on in Person A.

    Person B might have said, "Are you sad because you really want to have friends?"

2. If you circled this we are in agreement. I hear Person B empathically receiving what Person A is expressing.

3. I didn't circle this one because I hear Person B giving advice rather than empathically receiving what Person A is expressing.

    Person B might have said, "Do you feel sad because you'd like to have more connection with your daughter?"

4. If you circled this we are in agreement. I hear Person B empathically receiving what Person A is expressing.

5. I hear Person B taking responsibility for Person A's feelings rather than empathically receiving what is going on in Person A.

    Person B might have said, "Are you mad because you'd like more opportunities to help out?"

6. I hear Person B assuming that he/she has understood and then talking about his/her own feelings rather than empathically receiving what is going on in Person A.

    Person B might have said, "Are you feeling frustrated and needing more help with this subject?"

7. I hear Person B explaining rather than empathically receiving what is going on in Person A.

    Person B might have said, "Are you upset because

you'd like to see that everyone is treated fairly here at school?"

8. If you circled this we are in agreement. I hear Person B empathically receiving what is going on in Person A.

9. I hear Person B giving his/her opinions rather than empathically receiving what is going on in Person A.

    Person B might have said, "Are you upset and want some time to yourself to sort out your feelings?"

10. If you circled this we are in agreement. I hear Person B empathically receiving what is going on in Person A.

CHAPTER 4

Creating Partnership Relationships Between Teachers And Students

Partnership in Setting Objectives and Evaluation

In most schools, Domination schools, the role of teachers is to control the actions of students. It is assumed that teachers know what students need to learn and how students are to behave. On the basis of this knowledge teachers have the right to use "power-over" tactics (reward, punishment, guilt, shame, duty, obligation) to control the actions of students. And on the basis of this assumption, the school authorities establish learning objectives unilaterally. This leaves most students seeing only the possibilities of submission or rebellion, and teachers who are not altogether comfortable with this "power-over" role, feeling powerless to effect change.

But if we are to prepare students to create and maintain Life-Enriching organizations, I suggest we provide the opportunity for students to relate as partners with teachers and administrators. One manifestation of this partnership involves mutually establishing learning objectives.

Objectives with Life-Enriching Purposes

In order for objectives to be established mutually, it is necessary for teachers to clearly communicate how the lives of students will be enriched by pursuing the objectives they choose. This is critical, because Life-Enriching Education requires that actions of teachers and students be motivated by the intention to enrich life and not by fear of punishment or hope for an extrinsic reward (a high grade or a college scholarship, for example), and certainly not simply by some edict that implies that people in authority know what is good for us.

So am I advocating a school where the students study whatever and whenever they choose, a policy of total permissiveness? No more than I am advocating the continuation of the Domination system.

Perhaps there is no clearer way of differentiating between Domination, permissive, and Life-Enriching Education than by noting how learning objectives are determined:

- In Domination Education the teacher's objectives are pursued without the commitment of the student being necessary.

- In permissive education the student's objectives are pursued without the commitment of the teacher being necessary.

- In Life-Enriching education only those objectives that are mutually agreed upon by the teacher and student are pursued.

The process of the teachers and students mutually establishing objectives might begin with the teacher recommending an area of study and explaining the needs that the teacher predicts would be fulfilled by pursuing this area of study. If the student sees the value of the proposed course of study and agrees, mutual objectives have been reached. Or mutual objectives might be reached by the student suggesting an area of study that the teacher is willing to support.

The dialogue skills described in Chapters 2 and 3 are essential for teachers to be able to arrive at mutual learning objectives with their students. To maximize commitment from students to objectives, teachers must not only be sincerely aware of the Life-Enriching nature of the objectives recommended, but they must also be able to communicate how the objectives will be Life-Enriching to the students.

If and when students are unwilling to pursue certain objectives, teachers need these communication skills to help them understand the reasons for the student's unwillingness, so the teachers can determine whether there are ways of making the objectives more appealing; or through this understanding the teacher might come to see that other objectives would be better for the student to pursue than the ones originally advocated by the teacher.

Looking back over the educational objectives that professional educators determined would be helpful to me through the years, I would say they didn't predict very well. I do not see my life as having been significantly enriched by the majority of subjects that were offered. In retrospect, I can see many areas of learning I would have preferred to pursue that I believe would have served me better than those chosen for me.

Of course, it is much easier for the teachers and students to mutually establish objectives when schools are structured to support them doing so. If the administration has established a fixed curriculum, two alternatives exist for the teachers and students. They can mutually decide to ignore the fixed curriculum, acknowledging the negative consequences this might entail (for example, not doing well on achievement tests). Or they can mutually decide to pursue the fixed curriculum so as to avoid the negative consequences. Perhaps they can come up with some creative ways to teach and learn the fixed curriculum.

Students Have Always Had a Choice

To involve students as partners in setting objectives is not as radical as it might seem at first. Whether or not the right of students to be partners in determining their objectives is recognized, the students still have the choice. It has been my experience that more will choose to pursue the objectives offered by teachers and administrators when these objectives are presented as recommended options (assuming, of course, that the objectives have life-enriching possibilities) than when they are presented as something that must be done.

In other words, the difference between Life-Enriching Educational programs and Domination Educational programs is not that a choice of objectives is present in the former and not in the latter. The difference is that this choice is acknowledged and respected in Life-Enriching Educational programs but obscured in Domination Educational programs.

I had an interaction with the principal of a high school in a large city in the United States who was extremely upset when I introduced the possibility of students being partners in decision- making about their learning. He protested that there were simply some choices that students weren't allowed to make. I asked for an example.

He said, "In this state it is the law that students attend school until they are 16 years old. Therefore, they have no choice as to whether or not they attend school."

I found this rather humorous. Why was I at his school in the first place? The board of education had hired me to work with the schools in their city that had a thirty percent or greater unexplained absent rate each day. They hoped that I might provide the staff of these schools with ideas for how to make education more appealing to the students. Though the principal claimed that the students could not choose whether or not to attend school, at least thirty percent of the students were aware they had that choice.

During a break later in the day, one of the teachers came to me and said, "If you want to see something funny, you need to come into our school and watch the students laugh when the principal announces over the public address system that students must come to school every day. The thirty percent who need to hear the message aren't here."

Teachers' Fears of Student Involvement in Objective Setting

Some teachers and administrators in Domination programs are shocked when I suggest students be brought in as equal partners in objective setting. I find teachers particularly concerned about involving students for two reasons. The first comes from their fear that the ignorance of students may interfere with their knowing what is best for them.

For example, I have heard from first grade teachers, "I do not see how you can set mutual objectives with first graders; they do not know enough about the possibilities to make effective choices," and I have heard from college instructors, "I do not see how you can set consensual objectives in technical subjects with students who know nothing about the field." I do not see student ignorance as just cause for the teacher unilaterally establishing objectives. If teachers believe strongly in a certain objective, I would like to see them responsible for educating students regarding its importance to the point that the students are willing to actively commit themselves to it.

The second reason I find teachers concerned about establishing objectives mutually involves the possibility of a student rejecting values that the teacher considers crucial. This differs from the first situation in that no assumption is made of the student's ignorance; the student simply does not agree that the objectives are important. In this situation many teachers believe in the "spinach theory" approach. This approach can be roughly summarized as, "Although they do not want to eat spinach now, if I force them to eat it they will come in time to appreciate my making them eat it."

I am concerned about this type of thinking for two reasons. First, I question how many people do end up liking the "spinach" when introduced to it in this way. For every one anecdote I hear teachers relating about the students coming to like "spinach," I hear ten students relating how much they hated their teachers for forcing it on them.

Secondly, even if more students did learn to like "spinach" being introduced to it in this way, I would still be concerned that they might learn from the teacher's behavior that if you believe strongly about something, it is all right to "force it on someone else for his own good." I have seen too much damage come from such thinking to want to see it perpetuated in our educational institutions.

If a teacher is finally not able to arrive at mutual agreement with a student regarding the importance of certain objectives, I hope the teacher is open to any one of the following three possibilities:

1. That the objectives are not valuable to the student and hence should not be presented as essential or mandatory for that student.

2. That the objectives are valuable but the teacher has been unable as yet to clearly communicate the value to the student. In this case the teacher would recognize that further dialogue is needed.

3. That the teacher communicates both a belief that the objectives are important, and a desire for the student to reach them, but also that the student will not be punished if these objectives are not reached.

Examples of Mutual Objective Setting

In a first grade classroom in Montana, the teacher starts the semester by explaining to the students that she would like to teach them as much reading, math, science, and language arts as they would like to learn. She then demonstrates the range of possibilities of what each student could learn by the end of the semester. For example, she shows them a book that they could learn to read, and math problems that they could be able to solve, and in this way tries to clarify in each subject area what they might achieve.

Next the teacher suggests that the students let her know when they have decided what they want to learn. During this time the students are free to roam about and examine materials she has displayed in various parts of the room. As soon as students let her know what objectives they would like to work toward, the teacher establishes sub goals with that student.

For example, if the students say they would like to learn to read the book held up by the teacher, the teacher might ask them whether they know the sounds of consonants (demonstrating, of course, what she means by consonants). If the students don't know the consonant sounds, they and the teacher might agree on an immediate objective of learning six consonant sounds.

A second example of arriving at mutual learning objectives involves an undergraduate political science course in a university in Missouri. The teacher often has as many as three hundred students in this class, so establishing individual learning objectives could be enormously time-consuming. The first day of class the teacher distributes a sheet listing twelve different objectives. The students are encouraged to select any one of the twelve objectives that appeals to them, indicate their choice on a piece of paper, sign it, and return it to the teacher. This paper serves as a contract between the teacher and student, representing that they have mutually agreed upon objectives. If students are not actively interested in any of the twelve suggested objectives, the teacher requests that they come in for a private conference to consider additional objectives more to their interest.

Hearing the Need Behind the "No."

In order to arrive at mutual objectives, it is often necessary for the teacher to hear the need being expressed when a student says "No" or "I don't want what you are offering." If teachers have Nonviolent Communication skills, they sense the needs behind such statements. Often such messages express, "I am afraid of failing and have a need to protect myself from the pain I have experienced when I have not been able to learn in the past," or "I am suffering from personal troubles and have a need for understanding. Until I get this need met I have little energy to pursue any learning."

Once the teacher has clarified the need behind the "No" the teacher will be better able to meet that need in a way that allows the student to willingly pursue the learning activities suggested by the teacher.

And, of course, the teacher needs to always be open to the possibility that the "No" could mean that the student's needs would not be met by what the teacher is offering and it might be to both the teacher's and student's benefit to find alternatives to what the teacher has offered.

A teacher gave me this example of application of these communication skills in resolving a conflict with a student in her sixth grade classroom. The situation occurred on the second day of school. The teacher had presented several math objectives. Everyone in the class had selected an objective to work on, except one boy who sat and sullenly looked out the window. The teacher recalled the following dialogue that occurred between the student and herself.

Teacher: You seem bored and disinterested in the math objectives I suggested. It seems you would like to do something else.

Student: (Angrily) Math is stupid!

Teacher: Sounds like you really hate math and want to do something more helpful to you.

Student: Yeah.

Teacher: I'm disappointed in myself. I wanted to make math appealing, but I can see I didn't make it appealing to you.

Student: I don't see why we have to do math anyway.

Teacher: Are you needing to see the importance of something before you study it? You don't see any reason for doing math?

Student: Yeah.

Teacher: I'm confused now because I'm not certain whether you can't see how the math could be useful or whether you just don't like doing math. I'd like to know which it might be.

Student: It's just too hard.

Teacher: Are you saying you're frustrated and need more help to understand how to do the problems?

Student: Yes, and it's boring.

Teacher: So you get bored with it and want some way of making it more exciting.

Student: Yes.

Teacher: I'm confident that we could make it easier and more fun and I'd like to try.

Student: How?

Teacher: I'll need your help. I would need you to tell me any time the work becomes boring or difficult. Then we could experiment together to find ways of making it easier and more understandable.

Teacher: (Trying to empathize with student's nonverbal behavior) You still seemed doubtful.

Student: What if you're busy?

Teacher: So you want to know how we'll handle that?

Student: Uh-huh.

Teacher: In that case I would want you to do some other work that you were able to do until I have time. I wouldn't want you to work on math if you were stuck.

With this reassurance that the teacher would do her best to adjust the work to fit the student's level of competence and do her best to make the work interesting, the student was willing to commit himself to working toward an objective in math.

I do not mean to imply by this example that mutual resolutions always end by students doing what the teacher wants. As with all Life-Enriching interactions, what makes the resolution mutual is the teacher's consciousness that the objective is not to get the student to do what the teacher wants, but to create the quality of connection that will allow both the teacher and the student to get their needs met.

In situations where the teacher and student mutually agree to pursue the student's, rather than the teacher's, desires in a conflict situation, I have frequently seen teachers interpret this possibility as the teacher "giving in" or the student "winning." Such an interpretation is quite distressing to people who believe it is one's "duty" as a teacher to see that students do what is "good for them" (meaning that students do what the teacher wants). But I believe that teachers "lose" only when they submit to a resolution against their will, not when they are influenced to change their position after understanding a student's feelings and needs.

Exercise 6

Hearing the Need Behind "No"

In order to create mutual objectives and an atmosphere of mutual respect, rather than to impose our wishes on others, it is helpful to practice hearing the needs people are saying "Yes" to when they say "No" to our requests. Please circle the number in front of any statement in which Speaker B is able to hear the needs of Speaker A when Speaker A says "No."

1. *Person A (student):* "No. I'm not going to spend my free time helping her with her work."

   Person B (teacher): "We all need to help each other."

2. *Person A (student):* "I don't have to salute the flag."

   Person B (teacher): "If you don't, you'll have to go explain yourself to the principal."

3. *Person A (parent):* "I won't make my daughter do something she doesn't believe in."

   Person B (teacher): "It sounds like you want to support your daughter in being honest and true to herself.'"

4. *Person A (school principal):* "No, you can't eliminate letter grades in your class."

   Person B (teacher): "I can't keep participating in a system that ranks kids and contributes to stress and ruthless competition."

5. *Person A (student):* "I won't work on a group project."

   Person B (teacher): "Just give it a try."

6. *Person A (student):* "This assignment is so stupid. I won't do it."

Person B (teacher): "Do you want to make sure that the work you do has meaning for you?"

7. *Person A (student):* "I won't say I'm sorry when I'm not."

   Person B (teacher): "I'm afraid you'll be sorry if you don't."

8. *Person A (parent):* "I'm not willing to sit and listen to you tell me what's wrong with my child."

   Person B (teacher): "It sounds like you'd like more balance in our conversation, and might like hearing some things I admire and appreciate about your child as well as what is concerning me?"

9. *Person A (student):* "You're not going to catch me reciting poetry."

   Person B (teacher): "Do you think it's not cool?"

10. *Person A (student):* "Coloring in maps is so boring."

    Person B (teacher): "Would you like to find a different way to learn geography?"

Here are my responses for Exercise 6:

1. I didn't circle this one because I see Person B lecturing Person A with the intention to induce guilt rather than hearing what's going on in Person A. I guess that Person A needs respect for his autonomy and support for how he chooses to spend his time.

2. I see Person B making a threat rather than hearing what's going on in Person A. My guess is that Person A needs to protect her/his autonomy.

3. If you circled this we are in agreement that Person B is attempting to hear the needs of Person A.

4. I see Person B stating his/her opinion in such a way as to imply that Person A is wrong rather than hearing Person A's needs. I guess that Person A needs accountability and efficiency.

5. I see Person B responding with a suggestion rather than hearing Person A's need. I might guess that Person A needs protection from some frustration or dissatisfaction similar to what she has experienced in a previous group project.

6. If you circled this number we are in agreement. I see Person B hearing what Person A is valuing.

7. If you circled this number we are not in agreement. I hear Person B suggesting a threat and attempting to coerce by inducing fear rather than hearing Person A's needs. I might ask, "Do you need empathy for the pain you are experiencing?"

8. If you circled this we are in agreement. I see Person B

hearing the needs of Person A.

9. I see Person B probing and asking for an opinion rather than hearing the needs of Person A. A response that would indicate that Person B is listening for Person A's needs might be, "Are you wanting to protect yourself from painful feelings, like embarrassment or fear?"

10. If you circled this we are in agreement. I see Person B attempting to hear the needs of Person A.

The Most Important Part of Learning

I once participated in a psychotherapy class with Carl Rogers and learned a powerful lesson about the value of student involvement in setting learning objectives in the first ten minutes of the course.

Rogers began the class in a way that was unfamiliar to me. Instead of coming in and directing the learning process, he simply sat and waited for us to express what we wanted from the course. One of my classmates expressed dissatisfaction with Roger's non-directive teaching saying that he paid tuition to learn what Rogers had to offer and wanted to know why Rogers wasn't presenting information to us about psychotherapy. Rogers sincerely listened to the student's dissatisfaction and responded, "I believe that persons, regardless of how knowledgeable or creative they might be in a particular field, probably have no more than one or two ideas which are uniquely theirs. I could present to you the one or two concepts about psychotherapy for which I am given credit within five minutes. Then what would we do for the rest of the semester?"

Roger's statement apparently stimulated irritation within the student, who responded, "Yes, I agree that no one knows everything about a subject. But you know better than we do what has been done in the field and know better what is worth learning."

Again Rogers listened intently to what the student said and then responded, "It might be so that I have a better grasp of what has been done in the field of psychotherapy than you do. And maybe I have a better grasp of what is usually taught in this area. However, I am reluctant to decide by myself what is important for you to learn because I believe that the most important aspect in learning is to choose what is worth learning. If I alone make that choice, every day I would be reserving the most important part of learning for myself."

That lesson has stayed with me over the years and it helps me remember the value of bringing students in as partners in determining what is worth learning.

Students' Fears of Student Involvement in Objective Setting

It is not uncommon for students who have already gone through many years in Domination Schools to feel uncomfortable when given the opportunity to help establish their own learning objectives. "Listen," one of them will say, "I don't want all this negotiation with you. Tell me what I need to learn."

So when I am teaching and hear such a comment, I first offer that student empathy for his discomfort. Then I suggest that he try to enjoy a new and radical approach that I am going to try. I say to the class, "I'd like to see a show of hands. How many of you are here because you know what the subject is and you really want to learn it?" That will be Group A. "And how many of you are here because you're afraid of what's going to happen to you if you're not here?" That will be Group B.

Now, I'd say in almost all of the schools that I've been working in, about 3/4 of the students fall into Group B. After the show of hands, I suggest that we not proceed with class until everybody is in Group A, but that no one join Group A out of a sense of fear or obligation. The conversations that then emerge between the two groups not only concern the values of the course materials, but also the students' and my personal values.

Some students never learn to appreciate this approach, or at least will not admit to it, but most grow to see its worth. Often the student who raised the original objection will be able to come up with the most compelling reasons for why this class will be Life-Enriching (even if he is unfamiliar with this concept) and will be better able to convince those in Group B to come over to Group A than I will.

Partnership in Evaluation

The partnership relationship between students and teachers in Life-Enriching Education is also reflected in choosing how to determine when learning objectives have been reached. This requires the ability to create measurable objectives and the means for evaluating whether they have been reached.

If a teacher learns to establish mutual objectives with students that are clear, attractive, and relevant, I see six consequences resulting, all of which enhance the student's autonomy and interdependence and support partnership between teachers and students.

1. When objectives are measurable and mutually established, the students become less dependent on the teachers. In fact, once students know exactly what the objectives are and how to measure when they have been reached, it is sometimes possible that the students can get there without any help at all from the teacher. Conversely, if the objectives remain only in the mind of the teachers, then the students have no alternative but to passively wait for instructions from the teacher.

2. When objectives are measurable and mutually established, evaluation can be objective rather than subjective. One of the benefits of stating objectives in terms of student behavior is that a criterion can be established to determine concretely if and when the objective has been reached. In the majority of cases, students can test themselves to see where they are in relation to where they want to go. This allows the teacher and the students to escape the arbitrary evaluation involved in the "grading game." Once the criteria have been mutually decided upon, the students keep working until they reach their objective.

3. When objectives are mutually established and measurable, I see the student as being able to play a more active role in self-evaluation. This follows from the advantages listed above. That is, once objectives are stated in clear measurable terms, the students are better able to evaluate their own performance and hence can play a more active role in evaluation.

4. When objectives are mutually established and measurable, the students have more of a chance to gain a sense of accomplishment. Once students knows what the objectives are and how to evaluate them, they can keep working until they have totally mastered the objectives. In contrast, I see it as quite possible for students to go through 12 years of school and never feel that they have completely mastered any objective, if objectives are vaguely defined and evaluation is arbitrary. All one has to do to get by in the majority of classrooms is to get a higher score on a test than other students. Thus, students can get an "A" in a class without feeling that they have really learned anything in that class. The "A" could be obtained merely by learning more than the other students did (or by having already known it before). I personally have never found receiving a high grade as meaningful as knowing that I have reached a learning objective of my own creation.

5. When objectives are mutually established and measurable students have more commitment to reach the objective than if the objective is created for them. I believe that the apathy characteristic in many classrooms can be largely traced to a lack of commitment by the students to the objectives toward which they are working. In fact, as has been mentioned, in many cases the students are not even clear as to what the

objectives are. Industrial psychologists have documented the degree to which morale and productivity are related to commitment to objectives. I believe it is a mistake to begin any course of instruction before the teacher is convinced that each student is committed to the proposed objective. When students are actively committed to objectives, I also see discipline problems greatly reduced. The more the goals of the student and those of the teacher coincide, the less problem of control I would anticipate.

6. When objectives are mutually established and measurable, the student and the teacher are protected against irrelevance. When the teacher tries to show the student how his life will be enriched by working toward an objective, the teacher soon finds certain areas of the curriculum that do not seem to meet the needs of the student. Perhaps they were relevant when they were established in the curriculum 50 years ago, but they may no longer be relevant today.

Unfortunately, finding that a subject is not relevant to students does not always mean that it will be removed from the curriculum. At times the rigidity of educational institutions leads to subjects being required even after they have lost all semblance of relevance. In such cases, as was described earlier, I see honesty to be the best policy with students. This honesty may be stated: "I would like to recommend the following objective for no other reason than that attaining it is highly valued within this school system. Although I can see no intrinsic value in learning it, I would suggest learning it in order to protect yourself in the present system. I would be most happy to explore with you ways in which we can make reaching this objective as pleasant as possible."

I would offer the following example of a teacher trying to establish mutual objectives with subject matter a student didn't see as Life-Enriching but that was required by the educational system. This dialogue took place in a seventh grade classroom for thirty students who were not achieving in a regular program. I helped design the program and trained the teacher who was selected to conduct it.

When the teacher and students were discussing what objectives the students might work toward, the teacher recommended that the students learn to multiply and divide fractions. One student asked why it was important to multiply and divide fractions.

The teacher answered, "There are some jobs that you are likely to do that require knowing how to multiply and divide fractions. For example, if you ever cook it helps in either cutting down or expanding the recipe. Also in carpentry it helps in either cutting down or expanding what you are building from scale drawings."

At this point the student said, "But I'm not going to be a cook or a carpenter."

The teacher thought about this for a moment and said, "Now that I think of it, I have not had a need to either multiply or divide fractions since I've been out of school." Thinking a while longer the teacher said, "However, I do know this. Problems requiring the multiplication and division of fractions are on most achievement tests, and if you don't do well on achievement tests you are likely to get stuck in low track classes in the school system.

Problems requiring the multiplication and division of fractions are also on many civil service examinations. If you don't know how to solve them it could hurt your chances of getting a job in the future." At this point the student questioning the objective decided that it would be worth his while to learn to multiply and divide fractions. Had he not chosen this objective, the teacher would have respected his choice and seen whether he could interest him in other objectives.

When teachers and students can see no Life-Enriching value to subjects required by the educational system within which they are functioning, another option would be for the teachers and students to work as partners in attempting to remove from the curriculum the objectives they see as irrelevant.

Accountability, "Yes," Grades, "No"

In Life-Enriching Educational programs, tests are given to determine whether or not objectives have been reached, and if not, the tests provide information about what the student still needs to accomplish. Tests are not given at the end of instruction solely to determine grades.

Reporting on a student's progress in a Life-Enriching Education classroom is done by describing the competencies that a student has developed. This can be done through a report card or parent conferences, if appropriate. If parent conferences are chosen I would prefer students to be involved in the conferences.

Grades are not given in Life-Enriching Educational programs. Instead, reports are presented about exactly what students are able to do at the end of the learning period that they were not able to do at the beginning.

I frequently hear the statement from teachers, "But we have to give grades in our system."

I understand the conditions they are referring to. I recall one time when I was teaching at a college in St. Louis. An administrator came to my office two days after grades were due and angrily demanded that I hand in my grades. I explained that I was choosing an alternative evaluation system.

The registrar was surprised by my response and said, "But you have to give grades." I said I was choosing not to give grades because to do so would be in conflict with my values. The administrator asked me to clarify what values of mine wouldn't be met by giving grades.

I explained that half of the students at the college were Black yet 80% of failing grades went to Black students. I said it wasn't in harmony with my values to participate in an evaluation system that discriminated on the basis of race.

I further explained that I see grades as unfair in that they seldom take into account the unequal levels at which people begin a course of instruction. If students begin the semester far above others in the class on achievement skills, they are quite likely to get a high grade (provided that they do not irritate the teacher personally), even though they may have learned little or nothing during the semester. Conversely, students who started the learning period far behind the others are likely to get a low grade even if they show considerable improvement.

I also pointed out that grades contribute to extrinsically motivating students and I wanted to be sure my students were doing the work solely because they saw the intrinsic value of doing so. I expressed my concern about the effect this extrinsic motivation had on students. I can think of no better way to make people unnecessarily anxious and other-directed than to establish vague, teacher-directed goals and then punish students with social disapproval (in the form of a low grade) when they do not reach the goals.

Then I told him that I saw the grading system communicating that competitiveness was to be valued above interdependence. In schools using grades competitively I see students learning that it is not only appropriate but actually expected that one climbs over others in order to attain a high grade. I said that I would prefer to see interdependence stressed in the classroom, to see students learn that their individual welfare is interwoven with the welfare of others. In such a classroom, the stress would not be on competing to get the grade but on everyone cooperating to see that all objectives are reached.

Finally, I explained that I understood that the purpose of giving grades was accountability, but I saw grades as being a very poor system of accountability. I told the registrar that I was preparing a description of what each student was able to do as a result of their time with me that they weren't able to do before. In this sense I pointed out I was being more accountable than teachers who simply handed in letter grades that told very little about what students had learned.

I was able to convince the registrar of the wisdom of my views. Other teachers, who have had less success in persuading administrators that grades are not in the students' best interests, have tried different approaches. Morrie Schwartz (of *Tuesdays with Morrie*), a professor at Brandeis University during the Viet Nam conflict, along with the rest of the Brandeis faculty, didn't want to give failing grades to any of his students because that could easily result in their being drafted and possibly killed. So everyone received A's.

Studies in the United States show that the A student learns the same amount each semester as the D or F student, if you measure growth from beginning to end. Why? The A students already know the material. Their parents prepare them, hire tutors, and provide enriching educational experiences that only the affluent can afford, so that their kids are the ones getting the A's. Those kids are the ones raising their hands right away; they're the ones with the answers.

But it only looks like we're teaching them.

I do not want to imply that our goal is to simply get away with not giving grades. As with any conflict in which we use Nonviolent Communication, the goal is not to get our way. We want to make human connections that result in everyone's needs getting met, and in the case of longstanding traditions such as grades, this dialogue between teachers who would prefer not to give grades and administrators who insist upon them can take a very long time. But as we communicate our preferences to not only the administrators but also to students, parents, and other teachers, we are slowly educating them, opening their eyes to new and wonderful possibilities, to our vision of schools where students learn willingly and eagerly, not just to earn A's or avoid F's.

NVC in Education

The Test

A High School teacher tells the following story.

My class is one of several "self contained" classrooms in the district. It is for the kids who do not fit into the regular High School program, mostly because of chronic aggressive behaviors or because they're so depressed they don't function very well. The class is a bit of a pressure cooker, with tempers often flaring at a moment's notice.

Before taking my first NVC class, I relied exclusively on a variety of behavior modification techniques to maintain order. This meant that I spent a good deal of my time bribing the kids with rewards and threatening them with punishments. While these techniques, particularly threatening punishment, often worked to get order in the moment, I had seen for a long time how they add to the seething resentments, anger, and low self-esteem that are so characteristic of these kids. Unfortunately, I didn't have any other tools to manage the classroom—until I discovered NVC.

When I first heard the NVC trainer say that all people are ever saying is "please" or "thank you," I laughed out loud. It was an impossible stretch of the imagination to hear the things my students say as only "please" or "thank you." But I guess I was desperate enough to try to make that stretch, because I very soon found myself hearing my students in a different way—actually hearing "please listen," or "please help" in their demands and angry outbursts. Hearing in this new way, and learning to express my own feelings and needs to my students has changed the tone of my classroom from one of constant tension to more openness and trust.

One of the first times I experienced this shift was when we were preparing for one of the semi-annual state mandated standardized tests. Most of my students score below grade level on these tests and hate taking them. In the past, I had the attitude, "This is something we just need to get through and complaining about it won't help." This time, like the other times, I felt the tension in the air, observed the tightness in their bodies, and an increased amount of irritability with each other. What was different was that I was able to sense more clearly what was going on beneath their actions. With my newfound NVC skills I was able to guess about what they were feeling and what needs of theirs were not getting met.

Silently I empathized with their unexpressed feelings and needs: "I imagine you are scared and want to protect yourself from the pain of failing again" . . . "I guess you are hurt and want to be acknowledged for the fullness of you rather than just being seen as a 'bad student'" . . . "I hear you are angry and guess it's because you want to protect your autonomy—to have choice about how you spend your time" . . . In addition, I was pretty sure that many of my students frequently felt hopeless about getting their needs met at school, or anywhere else for that matter. Having to endure standardized tests seemed to bring all of these painful feelings and unmet needs to the surface.

Understanding them in this way really opened my heart and caused me to pause when, in the midst of telling the class what our testing schedule would be for the week, one of the students suddenly shouted, followed by several others.

Student 1: Why do I have to take this stupid test?

Student 2: Yeah, give us one good reason.

Student 3: It's to show who's smart and who's stupid.

Student 4: Yeah, well, the ones who made up this test are the stupid ones.

Teacher (listening to their feelings and needs): Are you feeling irritated because you'd like clarity about how you would benefit from taking the test?

Student 1: Yeah, why do we have to take them? We know what the results are going to be. It's a stupid waste of time.

Teacher (reflecting his needs): I guess you'd like to know the reasons behind people asking you to do things?

Student 5: Not "ask" us to do. Make us do.

Teacher (hearing more feelings and needs): So you're angry, too, because you'd like to choose what you do here, and not be forced to do things.

Student 5: Yeah, here and everywhere else. What do we get to choose? We don't even get to wear the clothes we want to school.

Teacher (in a tone of voice that expresses inquiry): You're fed up with all the things that adults decide for you? You'd like more choice?

Student 5: It's stupid to even talk about it. There's nothing we can do.

Teacher (continuing to guess feelings and needs): It sounds like you're feeling pretty discouraged about even getting heard by adults?

Student 5: Yeah. Why waste my breath?

Teacher: So you feel hopeless and, I'm guessing, real sad when your need for understanding isn't being met?

Student 5: (Silently, he lowers his head, his eyes filling with tears.)

Everyone was quiet for a few minutes. There was a noticeable shift in the energy of the class, from tense and angry to soft and sad. I'm sure it was because I was able to just listen to them—with no resistance, argument, or pat answer. Then the first student who had spoken, asked his question again.

Student 1: So why do we have to take these tests? Do you know?

Teacher: The truth is, I don't really know why you have to take them. I've been told some reasons for the test, but I'm not as clear about them as I'd like to be, so I'd rather not talk more about it right now. I promise you that I will look into the reasons for these tests and get back to you. I want you to know why it is you are being asked to do things. I really want to be clear why I am asking you to do things. I also feel sad because autonomy is very precious to me and I want you to have more choice in your lives. I'd like to do something about that. So I appreciate very much that you opened up this discussion today and shared your needs and the feelings connected with them.

Following this exchange, I said to my students, "Obviously, there are a lot of painful feelings associated with taking these tests. There's also a lack of clarity about their purpose. I want to continue to address your needs and the confusion and other feelings connected to them. Is anyone doubting my desire to do this?"

When no one spoke up, I continued: "In the meantime, to make things easiest for all of us right now, I'd like to begin and complete this round of testing that has already been scheduled. Is there anyone who would not be willing to go along with me on this?" I remember I felt so astonished and grateful to see that no one was unwilling to take the dreaded tests that day.

Now, of course, I see that my students were always telling me how they feel. I was the one who acted differently that day, by taking the time to hear what they were saying, and by being willing to honestly express my feelings and needs to them.

I really got the power of NVC in education that day.

CHAPTER 5

Creating An Interdependent Learning Community

Secular Ethics

Students receive powerful learning experiences from the ways their classrooms and schools are organized. The organization of classrooms and schools can support the learning necessary for students to develop and maintain either structures that support interdependence or structures that support competition and Domination.

Life-Enriching Education structures the school as a community where each student is equally concerned about contributing to other students' reaching their learning objectives as they are about reaching their own. Not only does such a learning community provide learning which will be helpful to students as adults in creating and maintaining Life-Enriching family, work, and government organizations, but it also facilitates the development of what the Dalai Lama refers to as 'secular ethics':

Along with education, which generally deals only with academic accomplishments, we need to develop more altruism and sense of caring and responsibility for others in the

minds of the younger generation studying in various educa-
tional institutions. This can be done without necessarily
involving religion. One could therefore call this 'secular
ethics', as it in fact consists of basic human qualities such
as kindness, compassion, sincerity, and honesty.

Most of us would agree with the Dalai Lama that we need to support the younger generation in the development of more altruism and
sense of caring and responsibility for others. Yet we are living in a
culture that supports competing to see who comes out on top in an
unfair competition in which the privileged are almost guaranteed to
win. Our schools reflect this clearly. As I indicated in the previous
chapter, the students who get the highest grades are not necessarily
the ones who have learned the most. They are the ones who had
already learned what was being presented before it was presented
because their family's economic situation provided a head start for
them in learning the things that are studied in schools.

So I'd like to see the competitive classroom transformed into a
learning community in which all members are concerned not only
about their own learning but equally for the learning of everyone else.

Developing an Interdependent Learning Community

Schools and classrooms where interdependent learning communities are thriving usually encourage students who have
reached certain objectives to assist others wishing to reach these
objectives. Having students teach one another contributes to the
development of an interdependent learning community. Once students have reached certain learning objectives they are then in a
position to be able to support the learning of other students.

This can take many forms. To begin with, it can take a tutorial
form where students who have already developed a skill can teach
it to others. There is ample evidence that students can teach each

other as effectively as trained teachers can teach them. This is certainly not a new concept to those who work in a country school setting, in Montessori schools, or in other multi-age classrooms. In such settings where a wide age range of students might be found grouped together in one class, it has been commonplace to have students teaching one another.

When I observed such a classroom in an NVC based school in Israel recently, I noticed a boy being instructed by a girl who looked to be about his age. As I watched, I saw that while he was working on some problems she had given him, she turned to her right to receive some instruction in a different subject offered by another, older student. All the students in the class were involved in this giving and receiving of instruction except for four who were working with the teacher. They were students with special learning needs. The teacher had the time to address their needs because the other students were actively learning without her having to be involved.

By allowing for learning experiences in the classroom in which students can be engaged by working alone or with one another the teacher then is free to troubleshoot. Troubleshooting might involve private instruction, or it might mean sitting and talking to students who appear to need to talk with someone on a particular day more than they need to work on a specific learning task. Troubleshooting might also involve interacting with students who are not learning effectively in order to determine what their needs are.

I have heard some teachers worry about having students teach one another because they fear that this is unfair to the student who has to do the teaching. But most teachers agree that no one learns more about a subject than the person teaching it, and that the child who teaches stands to benefit as much as the one being taught. Teachers who practice this in the classroom have told me that the students doing the teaching gained considerably in their awareness of the learning process and this appeared to facilitate their own learning.

The Teacher as a Travel Agent

I have also heard teachers express the concern that assigning one child as a teacher of another could actually increase competitiveness, lead to just another kind of one-upmanship. But in a classroom where everyone has a different set of learning objectives, where there is no established hierarchy of achievement, it is quite possible for a student to be capable of teaching in one area but in need of instruction in another, and comfortably both offering and asking for help.

Maybe it's because I travel so much, and I have a lot of contact with travel agents, but in such a classroom, I like to think of the teacher as the travel agent and the students as the travelers. A travel agent doesn't tell me where to go. But sometimes, if I tell him my needs, he might recommend some places that I haven't thought of, and that I don't know about. So the teacher, like the travel agent, might offer some suggestions, might strongly encourage, but would never tell the students where to go. Meanwhile, one student-traveler might tell another about a wonderful place where he has been, and get that student excited about going there.

Another thing I like about the travel agent image is that the travel agent doesn't go on the trip with the client, so the trip doesn't depend on the travel agent's availability. In the Israeli school described above, during a specific period each day the students pick their own teachers, and 60% pick other students.

Studies in the United States show that a child who has just learned a skill can be a better teacher of that skill with other children, than a trained teacher. And why should that be surprising? The children speak the same language, they know each other, they feel safe with each other, and the experience of learning the skill for the first time is still fresh. So if a friend knows how to ride a bike, he can teach another friend how to ride a bike. Or if a friend knows how to add up arithmetic problems, she can show another friend how to do that.

And the travel agent doesn't expect all clients, even those who have the same objectives, to reach their destination at the same time, or to get there the same way. If somebody doesn't have much money, maybe he can go by train. Another might go by plane, and so on. The teacher can adjust the trip to fit the traveler. So if the student is having trouble with reading comprehension, until he gets that, she teaches him differently. If one of his objectives is to learn about something he has seen in a science book, she asks a student who can read, to read to him, rather than making him learning dependent on a skill he does not yet have.

So the travel agent doesn't tell you where to go, and doesn't go with you. But she assists you, offers some alternatives, and shows how these alternatives might be Life-Enriching.

Materials That Allow Students to Learn by Themselves

After the teacher and student have mutually established learning objectives, the teacher then works with students to obtain the information and materials they need to successfully fulfill the objectives. Ideally, the materials may be such that students often can use them by themselves. This involves the teacher identifying the prerequisite competencies or concepts that constitute readiness on the part of students to start working toward their objectives.

Next the teacher and students work together to identify and define the contributing concepts, the instructional activities, the target date, and the vocabulary the learner needs in order to reach the objectives. The teacher would then arrange these elements in the sequential order that best serves the student's progress toward the objective. Each element would be fully stated in a form that tells students exactly what they must know or be able to do and indicates the materials and learning experiences required for its mastery.

These "trip packs," using the travel agent image again, would be made available to the students, preferably without dependence on the teacher's initiation, and with a set of instructions telling the students how to use them. Teachers can prepare their own custom or special purpose learning units, and, of course, they can also use commercially produced materials. For the teacher with money budgeted for materials, there is now a plethora of such materials from which to choose. Or with assistance from students, volunteers, and parents, materials can be constructed so that students' learning is not always dependent on the teacher's availability.

Utilization of Students and Parents in Providing Materials

Students and their parents are resources that can be called on for help in preparing materials. Not only can students and parents save the teacher time and effort, but also in the process they can benefit from the experience.

In the seventh-grade classroom of a friend of mine, the students liked working with a commercially prepared reading kit. However, there was only one kit for the entire class. Therefore my friend suggested that the class make several kits of their own following the design of the commercially prepared kit, by using articles found in magazines. Enthusiastically, several of the students began working on this project. Initially my friend was concerned because the students constructing the kits were using articles that he anticipated would be too difficult for them to read. For example, they were selecting articles of personal interest on subjects such as drugs and many of these articles were culled from journals that supposedly were beyond the reading levels of the students. However, to the surprise of my friend, the students not only used these self-made kits to improve their reading but preferred them to the one commercially prepared kit.

I was once asked to attend a parent-teacher event for my youngest son's kindergarten class. The advertised purpose of the meeting was to acquaint the parents with the program. When we arrived we were told that parents and students learn best by doing. Therefore, rather than have the parents passively listen to the teachers tell us about the program, we were told that we would be given an opportunity to learn about the program by making materials for it. The teachers had assembled a lot of raw materials (none of which were expensive) such as old magazines, glue, paint, colored cardboard, scissors, etc. The teacher then gave instructions for the construction of certain learning materials. As the teacher gave the instructions, the use that would be made of these materials was described.

I was put to work on a detail making sets of concept cards. I was to look through magazines, find four pictures that went together (for example, pictures of four different types of vehicles—car, plane, boat, train) and one that did not go with this set (for example, a picture of an orange). These pictures were each to be pasted onto a 3 X 5 index card. The back of the card of the one that did not belong with the others (the orange in the example given) was to be colored red.

We were told that sets such as these would be used to help our children learn different concepts. The students would be given the sets of cards, would place the one in each set that did not belong on top, and then check to see if they were correct by seeing if the one on top had a red back. In this way we learned actively about the program and the teacher was able to capitalize on this voluntary labor to amass a large store of materials in a relatively short time.

Volunteer Tutoring Services

By volunteer services, I have in mind primarily the use of parents, grandparents, and other neighborhood personnel as supporters in the learning community. These people, I believe, could be of considerable help in reaching students who are not able to learn through procedures outlined previously. I know of one residential treatment center for "emotionally disturbed" children that uses elderly citizens as tutors.

The experience to date has been rewarding for both young and old. The principal of the school reported to me that often elders have the patience that so many of these young persons require, and also have the time to devote to them.

The Geographical Community as a Learning Resource

Another source that can be drawn upon to support the learning community is the geographical area in which the school is located. I observed a good example of how geographical community resources can be involved in teaching students in the Parkway Program in Philadelphia. In this program the "school" is viewed as the city itself. Courses can be held anywhere in the community where significant learning might go on. Thus students might go to the zoo for courses, or to the art museum, local industries, etc.

These resources were contacted by the school authorities to determine their willingness to provide personal supervision, resources and facilities, and were viewed as partners in the educational process, not mere locations for enjoyable but isolated field trips.

The Travel Agent in Action

In the previous chapter I described a first grade classroom in Montana and outlined the process the teacher follows to establish mutual objectives with each student. I left the description at the point at which a few students have indicated to the teacher that they would like to learn six consonant sounds.

I would now like to describe what happens from that point because I think it will demonstrate some of the suggestions made in this chapter.

Upon arriving at the objective of learning six consonant sounds with the students, the teacher has several options open.

1. The teacher can determine whether she has games that the student can play, the purpose of which is to help students learn the consonant sounds (there are several such games commercially available). If these games need more players she may ask the rest of the class if anyone else is interested in learning the consonant sounds as a means of getting started in reading.

2. The teacher can determine whether she has programmed materials that the students can use to learn the consonant sounds.

3. The teacher can determine whether there are other students in the class who know the consonant sounds under consideration who would be willing to teach them to the students wanting to learn them.

4. The teacher can determine whether she herself has the time to teach the sounds to the students.

The teacher in question related to me that usually by the second day of class all of the students have decided on at least one objective and have started working toward it. I would like to follow up on the students who committed themselves to learning six consonant sounds. Let us assume that they choose to play a Consonant Lotto Game and now believe they know the six consonant sounds. They might approach the teacher saying, "We think we know the sounds now."

If the teacher has not developed procedures for students

measuring their own performance, she might then check to see whether the students have learned the consonant sounds. If they demonstrate proficiency in the sounds, the teacher notes this in their folders. As soon as the students learn to print they are responsible for keeping their own folders up to date by keeping a record of every objective they reach. Twice each semester the students will be expected to arrange a conference between their parents, the teacher, and themselves. The students preside at this meeting using their folders to review for the parents and teacher what they have been able to learn to date.

All the students in this classroom follow the same procedure described. As students finish working on an objective, they or the teacher records it in their folders, another objective is arrived at mutually with the teacher, and the process is repeated. If the teacher sees that certain students are doing an inordinate amount of work in reading but avoiding math, she would express concern about this imbalance and encourage the students to pursue more math objectives. However, at no time does the teacher impose objectives on the students.

The parents have been pleased with the freedom and flexibility of this approach to teaching. They were also pleased with how much their children learned and enjoyed learning. In fact, the parents were so pleased that they petitioned the school board to allow their children to remain with the teacher for a second year in order to continue the program. I am happy to report that the school board so valued the results the teacher obtained that they have asked her to counsel other teachers who want to arrange their classrooms in this manner.

I fully realize that I am not presenting anything you have not heard many times before. And I can already hear your objections, depending on where your school is and what your resources are.

If I have somehow led you to believe that I think the shift from a Domination class or school to a Life-Enriching class or school is an easy one, let me assure you that is not the case. I have personally been involved in the struggle and have been disappointed by enough failed attempts to establish such schools to know how challenging it can be. Swimming against the current, going against the established, traditional system, is never easy.

What gives the idea of Life-Enriching education that I propose a chance of working isn't the technical aspects of it, the self-correcting materials and peer tutoring and travel agent teacher I have described. What is needed to make these techniques work, not in just a few isolated schools but in all schools, is what lies at the heart of Life-Enriching Schools and all Life-Enriching organizations: the goal to help one another, to make life more wonderful for one another, as evidenced in an interdependent learning community.

Using Nonviolent Communication skills, constantly asking of students, teachers, administrators, and ourselves, "What are you feeling and needing?" we actually can meet everyone's needs. No longer will the goal be merely to reduce violence and vandalism, to keep kids in school as long as possible, to get higher scores on the proficiency tests than the kids in the next county do, to get more kids into college than we did last year, or to improve our students' showing on the SAT exams.

No longer will students and teachers alike be given only two choices, to submit or rebel. When there is only one goal, to get everyone's needs met, classrooms and schools can be transformed. Because what we discover is that everyone's needs are the same.

CHAPTER 6

Transforming Schools

The Problems at Hand

We are obviously in need of radically different organizations than those that now control the quality of life on our planet. Millions of people are starving each year even though the planet provides enough food for everyone. We live in the midst of horrifying psychological, physical, and institutional violence.

I am in agreement with psychologist George Miller when he writes, "The most urgent problems of our world today are the problems we have made for ourselves. They have not been caused by some heedless or malicious inanimate Nature, nor have they been imposed on us as punishment by the will of God. They are human problems whose solutions will require us to change our behavior and our social institutions."

Life-Enriching Education focuses on how teachers can provide learning opportunities that will empower students to be an active force in solving these human problems. They can learn how to enrich their own lives and help others enrich theirs.

Domination Organizations

How did we come to the human problems that create the unnecessary human suffering and violence plaguing us? In her books *The*

Chalice and the Blade and her recently published *The Power of Partnership*, cultural historian and evolutionary philosopher Riane Eisler shows how what she identifies as the struggle between the partnership model and the dominator or domination model goes back thousands of years. Riane Eisler, who personally knew the horror of having to flee the Nazis as a child, has shown in her study of 30,000 years of human evolution (*The Chalice and the Blade*, 1987) how our problems emerged from the conquest and suppression of an earlier partnership culture by the domination culture in prehistory.

Drawing from Eisler's work, author and theologian Walter Wink also maintains that for about 10,000 years over much of our planet, human organizations have been functioning as "Domination organizations," controlling our spirituality, social structures, education, and human development (*The Powers That Be*, 1999). Wink defines Domination organizations as characterized by unequal distribution of resources and privileges, hierarchical power relations, and the use of violence to maintain order—systems in which a few people dominate many. We have these systems represented in the family, schools, religious organizations, work organizations, and the government. They all operate by the same rules.

Like Eisler, Wink further claims that such systems are based on a spirituality that portrays humans as essentially selfish and violent. Given that, we need to have Domination systems in which the least vile of us gets to control the others. Over the centuries, there has been more than a little bit of argument about who was going to be at the top of the list.

These people get to control others through the use of power-over tactics—punishment and reward, basically. They get to punish those who don't obey. That's the only way to educate people, to teach them a lesson, to teach them how bad they are, and who deserves what. This depiction of human beings justifies domination and control by those claiming superiority.

Wink is obviously not describing only totalitarian governments such as that of Nazi Germany when he writes of Domination systems. Even in the United States, we can see abundant examples of privileged groups of people sitting in positions of power, getting the best jobs, living in the best neighborhoods, and of course getting the best educations, with an air of entitlement that makes equal opportunity appear a lie.

Once we are aware of the power of Domination systems, it is easier to see that a transformation to Life-Enriching systems offers a better opportunity to meet the needs of all our citizens. I would like to educate this and future generations of children to be able to create organizations whose goal is to meet human needs, to make life more wonderful for themselves and each other. From that awareness, we can use the education of our children as a place to start.

Conflict Resolution

Two key issues in any school are how order is to be maintained and how conflicts are to be resolved. One of the components necessary for creating a Life-Enriching School is the skill of resolving conflicts in mutually satisfying ways. In Domination Schools the teachers and administrators decide on the basis of their experience that they "know what's best" for the student and make rules and regulations enforced by punishment and rewards. In this method of establishing rules and regulations the teachers and administrators may or may not consult with students. However, the teachers and administrators ultimately make the decision unilaterally, basing their right to do so on their expertise and experience.

In Life-Enriching Education, whatever rules and regulations are needed to maintain order are decided on through dialogue by the staff and students working together, being respectful of everyone's needs. This process does not involve anyone giving in, giving up, or compromising.

To maintain order and resolve conflicts in this way requires the staff and students to be competent in Nonviolent Communication skills. Staff and students need to be literate in connecting with one another's feelings and needs. After this quality of connection is reached, both sides engage in problem solving to find actions that can be taken that will fulfill all parties' needs.

It is important that before anyone agrees to carry out these actions that she checks inside to be sure she is motivated to act with the sole purpose of fulfilling needs, with no trace of doing anything to avoid punishment, guilt, or shame. Nor would she want to act out of a sense of duty or obligation, or in order to get a good grade or any other extrinsic reward.

Those who object to maintaining order and resolving conflicts in this way often sound like this: "Well, these kids have got to learn respect for authority! That's what we've got to do, to get these kids to respect authority!" And I usually respond, "Do you want to teach kids to respect authority, or to fear what you can do to them when you're in a position of authority?" Many of us, educated in a Domination System, are not aware of the distinction between the two.

I would define respect for authority in this way: in a classroom, if the teacher knows something that the students value, and she offers to teach it to them in a non-coercive way, they will learn to have respect for her authority. But she has earned that respect, not demanded it. The student is the final authority about whether or not the teacher has authority, a truth which students clearly demonstrate every day. Fear of authority masking as respect for authority is easy to get; just give the people with titles the legal power to mete out punishments and rewards.

Another way to describe this distinction is to explain the difference between self-discipline and obedience. If obedience is what you want, punishment and rewards work well. A dog is taught obedience that way. A cockroach can be put in a T-maze, given some food if it turns right, an electric shock if it turns left, and taught obedience. But if what you want is self-discipline I suggest you don't use any coercive tactics, because they get in the way of self-discipline. A self-disciplined student or staff member acts out of a certain consciousness of his own values, of how what he is doing will contribute to his own and others well-being, not out of a desire for reward or a fear of punishment.

Many teachers feel helpless when told not to motivate students using punishment, reward, guilt, or shame, or a sense of obligation to duty. What's left, they ask? What is left are connections between people and a desire to contribute to one's own self-fulfillment and the well-being of others. In my experience, these basic human needs can be met by learning to use the skills of Nonviolent Communication. We share what is valuable to us, why we would encourage others to consider it, and listen to their feelings and needs in return.

Notice that this requires that teachers be fluent in Nonviolent Communication even when the children they teach are often coming from Domination system backgrounds. So self-discipline as opposed to obedience (or disobedience) doesn't happen overnight. Very often the first weeks in a school attempting to become a Life-Enriching School can be chaotic.

I was once asked to help establish a Life-Enriching School for students who had all either dropped out or been expelled from public school. We wanted to demonstrate that Life-Enriching Education could reach students that the public schools were unable to handle. My job was to prepare the teachers to work in this school.

For financial reasons I was limited to four days to prepare the teachers. As a result, I was not able to provide the depth of training I would have liked. These were not even professional teachers, by the way; because of budget constraints we had put in a call to universities for volunteers to teach in this school. So here were kids that the public school couldn't reach, and a group of people that were good-hearted volunteers, and I was given four days to train them.

Not surprisingly, therefore, some of the teachers did not understand how to establish rules and regulations and resolve conflicts as I had suggested.

I was out of town the first few days that the school was open. When I got back, the first message I received was from the principal, "Get down here quick! They're thinking of closing the school. It's chaos!" I rushed down to the school. The poor teachers looked like they had aged 20 years in less than a week.

When I heard what was going on from the principal, I said, "Bring about ten of the kids into a room with me, the ones that are creating most of the trouble, so we can get some order in the school."

Eight students, ages 11-14, were selected by the principal. I began by introducing myself to the students and the following discussion ensued.

> *MBR:* I'm very upset about the teachers' reports that things are getting out of hand in many of the classes. I want very much for this school to be successful. Can you tell me what's going on, and help me fix it?
>
> *Will:* The teachers in this school are a bunch of fools, man.
>
> *MBR:* I'm not clear, Will, what they are doing that leads you to say that. Could you give me an example?
>
> *Will:* No matter what the students do, they just stand around grinning like a bunch of fools.
>
> *MBR:* Are you feeling disgusted because you want more order in the school?
>
> *Will:* That's right, man. No matter what anybody does the

teachers just stand there smiling like fools. Like, he (pointing to one of the students in the group) came to school yesterday with a pint of whiskey in his back pocket. The teacher standing at the door saw it, and he just pretended like he didn't, and he's smiling, saying, "Good morning, good morning!"

At this point all of them jumped in to give me one example after another of how passive the teachers were.

MBR: Fine, thank you, enough, enough. You've answered my question, but now I want your help in creating order in the school.

Joe: The teachers ought to get a rattan (a stick carried by administrators in the public schools in that region to administer corporal punishment).

MBR: Joe, are you suggesting that you want the teachers to hit students when they bother others?

Joe: That's the only way they're (students) going to stop.

MBR: I'm discouraged if that's the only way. I'm worried about that way of settling things and want to learn other ways.

Ed: Why?

MBR: Several reasons. Like if I get you to stop horsing around in school by hitting you with a stick. I'd like you to tell me what happens if three or four of you that I've hit with sticks in class are out by my car when I go home.

Ed: (Smiling) Then you better have a big stick, man.

MBR: That's what bothers me about getting order that way. It turns us into enemies. Remember, when we invited you to attend this school, we said we wanted to create a school where everyone works together in a cooperative way. If we get order by hitting people, I'm afraid we'll not have the connections between teachers and students that I'd like us to have in this school.

Ed: You could kick the troublemakers out of school.

MBR: I'm discouraged with that idea, too. I want to show that there are ways of solving differences in school without kicking people out.

Will: If a dude ain't doin' nothin' except causing trouble, how come you can't send him to a "Do Nothing Room?"

MBR: I'm not sure what you' re suggesting, Will. Could you explain?

Will: Sometimes you come to school and you don't feel like doing anything except causing trouble. Maybe your father beat the hell out of you before you left for school. So you don't feel like doin' nothing except causing trouble. So have a room where someone can go until they feel like coming back and doing their schoolwork.

(I noticed that the other students were nonverbally showing understanding and approval of Will's suggestion.)

MBR: Are you suggesting, Will, a room we could ask people to go to if their behavior is keeping other students from learning?

Will: That's right. No use their being in class if they ain't doing nothing but causing trouble.

MBR: I' m excited about that idea as long as we can get across to the students who are keeping others from learning that we're not trying to punish them by asking them to go to the room, but simply trying to protect the rights of those who want to learn.

After further discussion, we all agreed that the students with me in that meeting would go to all the classrooms and suggest that we try out the following: If someone was too upset to do any school work and their behavior was interfering with the learning of others, the teacher would request that they go to a "Do Nothing Room" where they would stay until ready to come back to class without disrupting others.

I stressed the importance of the students making clear to the other students that the rule was Will's suggestion (rather than one created unilaterally by the teachers or administration). I also stressed the importance of making clear that the intention was to protect the students who wanted to learn and not to punish the students who were not in a mood to learn.

The students did a good job of making these two points clear to the other students and the plan worked beautifully bringing more order into the classroom. A room was designated as the "Do Nothing Room." If a student is disrupting others, the teacher (and sometimes the students being disrupted) would ask the student to go to the "Do Nothing Room." Actually there was plenty to do in the "Do Nothing Room" such as music for students to listen to, books to read, etc. We wanted to do everything we could to communicate that the intention of being sent to the room was not to punish.

A lot of good communication happened in the "Do Nothing Room." The students creating the disruptions in the classrooms were typically experiencing a good deal of inner distress that led to their disruptive behavior. The teacher was assigned to that room on the basis of his good listening skills, which were put to very good use.

The first two weeks the rule was in effect the "Do Nothing Room" was packed with students. However, all of a sudden there were fewer and fewer students whose behavior led to their being requested to go to the "Do Nothing Room."

Often, when I tell this story and I get to the part about the rattan, I hear, "Well of course, because that shows you, kids want to be punished when they do something wrong. That's how they know you care for them." I understand how people might believe this, when they see only two choices: order or chaos. Anarchy, no order whatsoever, is pretty scary, and if kids think their choices are permissiveness, the result of which is anarchy, or punishment and therefore order, my experience has been that even the student who is going to be hit the most would prefer the rattan to chaos. But fortunately, there is a third choice, mutually established rules.

When rules are established by the people who are going to be affected by them, not handed down unilaterally by some authority, and everyone sees that the intention is to protect, not to punish, these rules are more likely to be respected. This is true regardless of peoples' ages. Look how many of us adults speed on the highway.

Mediation

If participants in a classroom conflict are lacking the communication skills necessary to resolve the conflict, third parties can be enlisted as mediators. For example, in an Israeli school practicing the Life-Enriching principles outlined in this book, I observed two ten-year-old boys requesting a "peacemaker" (the name for mediators in the school). They had had a fight on the playground, weren't doing so well resolving it themselves, and so they chose to seek a peacemaker.

The peacemaker on duty that day was an 11-year-old boy. When everyone was seated the peacemaker requested of the first boy: Observation?

The first boy knew that this was a request for an observation about what behavior was not in harmony with his needs. He responded, "He pushed me down on the playground for no good reason." The peacemaker called to the boy's attention that "for no good reason" was an evaluation and not an observation. The boy corrected himself saying, "He pushed me down on the playground."

Peacemaker: Feelings?

Boy 1: I feel hurt.

Peacemaker: Needs?

Boy 1: I need to be treated with respect.

Peacemaker: Requests?

Boy 1: I want him to tell me what his reasons were for pushing me down.

The peacemaker then turned to the second boy and asked him to repeat the observations, feelings, needs, and requests that the first boy had expressed. He was able to do so quite easily. Had he not been able to do so the peacemaker was trained to help him reflect back accurately what the first boy had said. Then the peacemaker asked the first boy if he felt understood and he indicated that he did.

Then the peacemaker turned to the second boy asking him to clarify his observations, feelings, needs, and requests and then asked the first boy to reflect back what had been said. Once both boys had been understood by the other, the peacemaker asked the boys whether they were able to see a way of getting everyone's needs met. It took only a few minutes of problem solving until they found a mutually satisfying solution.

Then the peacemaker asked how both felt and the first boy answered, "I feel good. He was my friend before this happened and I would hate to lose him as a friend." At this point the two boys and the peacemaker returned to their classes.

NVC in Education

"You're Dead"

A counselor at a High School facilitates a weekly NVC practice group for interested students. One of the students in this group, Kim, came to the counselor's office one day in obvious distress. The counselor invited her to sit down and asked her what was going on. Kim said that Tess, another student at school (not in the NVC group), had just walked by Kim in the hallway and, looking straight at her, said, "You're dead." Kim said that she had had other tense interactions with Tess, but this one really scared her.

Counselor: Wow, Kim . . . I see you're shaking . . .

Kim: (nodding her head and taking some deep breaths to calm down) Yeah . . . I'm scared. What if she really means it?

Counselor: (listening empathically to what Kim's feeling and wanting) You're wondering what was going on inside Tess to say that? And you want to know if she's really thinking about hurting you?

Kim: She could. She's got friends. And she sounded really mad.

Counselor: (trying to get more clarification about the situation) I'm curious about what she was reacting to—do you know?

Kim: She's angry about something I said about her to some kids.

Counselor: Uh huh . . .

Kim: It's true I said it . . . but she says stuff about me, too. Lots of stuff! *(suddenly angry)* She has no right to threaten my life!

Counselor: (hearing Kim's feeling beneath the anger) It's really scary for you to hear that and think she might be serious?

Kim: Yeah! I don't want to get hurt!

Counselor: Yeah. . . *(now reflecting Kim's need)* you want to be safe.

Kim: Yeah. I just want to live my life, come to school, not have to watch my back all the time.

Counselor: Sounds like you'd like to feel safe enough so you can focus your attention on other things at school besides your safety . . . like schoolwork and friends and soccer . . . ?

Kim: Yeah . . . This is a total waste of time. I don't know how it got so out of control! I know I'm partly to blame because I do talk crap about her. I don't know why I do that. It's stupid.

Counselor: (translating Kim's judgment into feelings and needs) Sounds like you're feeling regret about your part in this and would like to do some things differently in the future?

Kim: Yeah. I really don't want to gossip about people. It just hurts everybody. Tess talks crap behind my back and I hate it.

Counselor: Sounds like you're seeing how painful it is for everyone when people talk about each other in these ways?

Kim: (nodding her head) Yeah. I really want it to stop

Counselor: (noticing that Kim has relaxed now that she has received this much empathy, she expresses her own feelings and needs) Hearing you say that, I feel relieved and pretty excited, because I'm confident you can stop this conflict with Tess by choosing to do things differently—using your words to heal instead of to hurt. It begins, as you know, with a desire to connect. So I'm wondering if you're ready to try and connect with Tess today? Or do you need more understanding first?

Kim: (pausing a moment to check in with herself) I think I'm ready. I'm scared, though, to talk with her. I'd like you to be there.

Counselor: I'd like to be there. I'd like to hear you tell her your feelings and what you want just like you told me. And I'm betting she needs some empathy first before she can really hear you. Are you up for connecting with her feelings and needs in this matter?

Kim: I'd like to try.

The counselor arranges for Tess and Kim to meet in her office later that day. Kim arrives first and is seated when Tess comes to the door and looks in. Tess glares at Kim, then walks in and sits on a chair that faces Kim, her shoulders slumped forward, her arms crossed in front of her, and her eyes fixed on the floor.

Counselor: I'm glad you both could make it. I'm guessing you're both a bit scared to be here right now, wondering how this is going to go? *(looking at Tess)* Tess, I'd like to first give you a little background. Earlier today Kim came to my office for some empathy, because she had a lot of feelings stirred up by what's going on between you. After getting the empathy she wanted, she said she wanted to talk with you. She asked me to be here to help you both hear each other the way you want to be heard. To get to the deeper feelings and needs you each have. The way I do this is by helping translate anything that might sound like blame or criticism into present feelings and needs. How does this sound so far?

Tess: (still looking down) Okay.

Counselor: Great. I'd like each of us to feel safe, so please-either one of you-speak up if at any time you're not comfortable with what's happening here. Okay? *(seeing them both nod their heads, she then turns to Kim)* So, Kim, will you start by telling Tess what you're feeling and what your needs are?

Tess: Okay. *(looking at Tess)* Tess . . . I'm feeling a little scared right now, but not as scared as I was today in the hall when you said "You're dead." I came to see Paula [the Counselor] because she helps me sort things out by listening to me. What I see now is I really want to stop the war between us.

Counselor: (reminding Kim to make a present request after saying this much, to see how Tess is receiving her message) So, Kim, what would you like back from Tess right now in relation to what you just said?

Kim: I guess I'd like to know how you feel when you hear me say this.

Tess: (looking up for the first time, eyes fixed on Kim) What you said about me was a lie and now everyone believes it.

[Note: Tess's response did not answer Kim's question about how she felt. Instead, Tess expressed her pain, making clear that what she needs right now is empathy.]

Kim: (shifting from expressing to listening) Sounds like you're angry about what I said. You want people to know the truth and not believe something bad about you that's not true.

Tess: Yeah. People are angry at me now, including my boyfriend, because of what you said.

Kim: It's awful when people close to you are mad at you. And frustrating when it's about something that's not true?

Tess: Yeah. Why did you say that, anyway?

Kim: (taking a couple of deep breaths to connect with herself) I wasn't sure if it was true or not, what I said about you. And why I said it? I think I was just hurting bad because of things you said and the way we were with each other. When I said it, I just wanted to hurt you back. . . You know what I mean?

Tess: Yeah. I know how it feels to hurt and want to hurt back. It feels better. . . for a while.

Kim: Yeah, I feel real sad about all the hurt for both of us. I wish I hadn't said what I did . . . and other stuff

I've said, too. I'd like to stop the fighting and see if we can get along.

Tess: So what about the lies people believe about me?

Kim: Would you like to talk about what we can do to clear them up?

Tess: Yeah. You think we can really do that?

Kim: (smiling now, with tears in her eyes) Yes. I really do.

This dialogue demonstrates how a very "charged", and possibly dangerous, situation can be defused in a relatively few exchanges of empathy and honesty. The level of trust and connection that was created in this conversation between Kim and Tess is common in NVC dialogues, though the process may take longer and involve more exchanges in some situations. As can be seen here, the connection can be made even when only one of the participants in the dialogue is familiar with NVC.

Avoiding Moralistic Judgments and Diagnoses

The process of communication that empowers people to resolve conflicts so that everyone's needs are met is hampered by teachers whom the Domination system has taught to make moralistic judgments and diagnoses about students. Moralistic judgments and diagnoses imply that something is wrong with students who aren't learning or cooperating, or in some other way are failing to act in harmony with the needs of the teacher.

I have noticed five types of diagnostic categories commonly used by teachers to explain the behavior of students in their classrooms who are not behaving as the teachers would like.

Diagnostic Category 1: "Learning Disabled" or "Special Needs"

I hear teachers using this diagnosis to describe students they interpret as unable to learn or who are not learning as rapidly as the teachers would like.

Diagnostic Category 2: "Behavior Disordered"

I hear teachers using this diagnosis to describe students they interpret as able to learn but lacking the motivation or self-control to learn. The implication is often that such a student has not been sufficiently disciplined at home, has "character" issues.

Diagnostic Category 3: "Emotionally Disturbed"

I hear teachers using this diagnosis to describe students they believe have the capacity to learn but who have emotional pathologies which keep them from learning, usually as a result of being in "dysfunctional families."

Diagnostic Category 4: "Culturally Disadvantaged"

I hear teachers using this diagnosis to describe students who they believe have the intellectual capacity to learn but whose cultural experience has not sufficiently prepared them to perform in school.

Diagnostic Category 5: "Hyperactive/Attention Deficit Disorder

I hear teachers using this diagnosis to describe students who have an abundance of energy and appear unable to concentrate on anything for an extended period of time.

Other students are delivered to a classroom teacher already so labeled. Parents may send a child to kindergarten with Ritalin in his book bag, because he was labeled at preschool as ADD-ADHD.

Anyone who goes through the schooling I went through comes to think there are such things as "special needs" students, and that there is such a thing as being good at math or not good at math, a poor reader or an excellent one. So many good students have a negative image of themselves that they are worried, do people think I'm stupid?

When we have our consciousness so focused on what people might think of us, and what we think of ourselves if we make mistakes, then any kind of learning is frightening. That's why about 15% of students follow the philosophy; you can't fall out of bed if you sleep on the floor. Many of those we call underachievers are so fearful of not getting things right, they have decided it's easier and safer not to do anything.

I agree with Kenneth Clark when he suggests that such diagnostic categories frequently lead to self-fulfilling prophecies. ". . . once one organizes an educational system where children are placed in tracks or where certain judgments about their ability determine what is done for them or how much they are taught or not taught, the horror is that the results seem to justify the assumptions.

The use of intelligence test scores to brand children for life, to determine education based upon tracks and homogeneous groupings of children impose on our public school system an intolerable and undemocratic social hierarchy, and defeat the initial purposes of public education. They induce and perpetuate the very pathology that they claim to remedy. Children who are treated as if they are uneducable almost invariably become uneducable. . . . Many children are now systematically categorized, classified in groups, labeled slow learners, trainables, untrainables, Track A, Track B, the 'Pussycats,' the 'Bunnies,' etc. But it all adds up to the fact that they are not being taught, and not being taught, they fail." Clark (*Dark Ghetto*, 1965, p. 128)

I find that teachers do not feel encouraged to see possibilities for developing their own constructive actions when such diagnoses are made. In fact, another of the dangers I perceive in such diagnoses is the unspoken assumption that the teacher, to protect herself from overwhelm, should "pass the buck" to others. For example, when students have been labeled as "learning disabled," a frequent implication is that they need to be referred to a special education teacher who is better prepared to deal with such students.

When students have been labeled as "emotionally disturbed," a frequent implication is that they need to be referred to a social worker, psychologist, or psychiatrist whose job it is to help them with their problems so that they can return to the classroom free to learn. If teachers received the classroom support they needed from a system that valued such efforts, they could be empowered to create a positive learning environment to accommodate students with a diversity of needs.

Protective Use Of Force

When teachers and students are able to empathically connect with each other's feelings and needs in a conflict situation, a resolution can usually be reached in which the needs of both parties are fulfilled, or at least the parties can agree in goodwill to disagree.

However, in some situations the opportunity to engage in such dialogue does not exist, and the use of force may be necessary to protect life or individual rights. For instance, a teacher may want to talk with students about something the students are doing which could be injurious to themselves or others, but the students are unwilling to talk. Or perhaps the threat of injury to people or property is immediate, and there is not time to communicate. In these situations, the teacher may choose to resort to force. If so, it is important that the teacher knows the difference between the protective and the punitive use of force.

One way to differentiate between the protective and punitive use of force is to examine what the person using force is thinking. A person using the protective use of force is not judging the other person in a moralistic way. Instead his thinking is focused on protecting the well-being of himself and/or others.

For example, if a young student is running toward the street, the thinking of the teacher who uses the protective use of force is solely directed to protecting the student by physically restraining him from running in the street. This can be done without using the punitive use of force, which might take the form of hitting the child or psychologically attacking him by saying something like, "What's the matter with you, how could you be so stupid?" or "You should be ashamed of yourself!"

Punitive action is based on the assumption that people do things that harm themselves and/or others because they're naughty and, as they grow older, downright evil. A corollary of this way of thinking is that to correct the situation we have to make the wrongdoer see the error of her ways, repent, and change, through some punitive action. But it rarely works this way in practice. Punitive action, rather than leading to the sought-after repentance and learning, frequently leads to the wrongdoer feeling resentful and hostile, and she may become even more resistant to changing her behavior.

The protective use of force is based on the assumption that people do things that harm themselves and/or others out of ignorance. This ignorance might be in the form of not knowing how one's actions are affecting others, ignorance of how to meet one's own needs without violating the needs of others, or culturally learned ignorance that justifies violating the needs of others (for example, to justify one's belief that others deserve to suffer for what they have done).

Another way to differentiate between the protective and punitive use of force is by examining the intention of the person using the force. The intention of someone using the protective use of force is to prevent injury or violation of someone's rights. The intention behind the punitive use of force is to cause individuals to suffer for their perceived misdeeds.

Exercise 7

Protective Use of Force
vs. Punitive Use of Force

A key distinction between the protective use of force and the punitive use of force is that the sole intention of the person using protective force is to protect, while the intention of the person using punitive force is to punish (by threatening or carrying out physical punishment or by attempting to induce shame or guilt.) In the following situations, circle the number in front of any action taken by the teacher that is a clear example of the protective use of force.

1. At lunch recess, the teacher sees one student hit another student. The teacher is afraid someone will get hurt so she tells the student she saw hitting to go immediately to the principal's office until she can come and talk with him.

2. A teacher asks a student a question and the student does not answer. The teacher thinks, "How rude! I'll show you!" and tells the student he has to stay after class.

3. A parent has come to the classroom to show slides of their family's trip to Brazil. During the slide show, one student makes loud noises that attract others' attention even after the teacher has asked him to stop several times. The teacher, feeling frustrated and wanting the rest of the class to be able to pay attention to the slideshow, tells the student to go sit in the hallway until the slideshow is over.

4. When a teacher notices that a group of students are poking each other with sticks, she tells them, "Stop right now before someone gets hurt. I want you to come sit down until you come up with a safe way to play together!"

5. A teacher says to a student, "All week I've been telling you to stop throwing the ball at other students, but I still see you doing it. You will spend the next two breaks in the classroom cleaning the chalkboard."

6. A teacher leaves the classroom for five minutes and returns to find the students running around instead of reading at their desks as she asked them to do. She says, "You don't seem to know how to stay in your desks so you will practice by staying at your desks for the first ten minutes of lunch recess."

7. A teacher says to the class that she's very disappointed in the number of low scores on the recent standardized test. She then returns the tests, announcing each student's score as she hands them their test. When she returns the tests with the lowest scores, she shakes her head disapprovingly.

8. A student is running very fast down the hall and bumps into a teacher along the way. The teacher stops him and asks him to sit down. She then explains the reason for the rule against running inside the school building, citing the injuries that had been caused by someone running in the hall.

Here are my responses for Exercise 7:

1. If you circled this number, we're in agreement that the teacher in this situation is most likely using her power to protect, not to punish—assuming that she trusts that the principal will not punish the child.

2. If you circled this number, we're not in agreement. The thoughts of the teacher reveal the kind of judgment that usually is associated with an intent to punish.

3. If you circled this number, we're not in agreement that this is a clear example of protective use of force. It is not clear to me what the intention of the teacher is given the information provided.

4. If you circled this number, we're in agreement that this is an example of the protective use of force.

5. If you circled this number, we're not in agreement. It is not clear to me what the intention of the teacher is given the information provided. I would assume that the intent was to punish.

6. If you circled this number, we're not in agreement. As in the previous situation, the teacher's intentions are not clear. I would assume that the intent was to punish.

7. If you circled this number, we're not in agreement that this is an example of the protective use of force. By publicly announcing the test scores and continuing to express her disappointment with the students who had low scores, I would interpret that she is attempting to punish these students by inducing guilt.

8. If you circled this number, we're in agreement that the teacher's thinking is in harmony with the protective use of force.

Creating Sustaining Teams

Most Americans are well aware of the inequities and deficiencies in our public schools that seem to keep our "underprivileged" exactly that, schools from which students graduate unable to read, unemployable, destined for poverty and/or criminal activity, if they graduate at all. The cries for educational reform rise and fall, and have seldom been louder than at this moment.

Now, one of the mistakes I've made historically was to assume that if we had a school where students learn more academic skills and more quickly, where there is less violence and more cooperation, that's all there would be to it. The whole world would say, "Hey, look at that program; that's all we have to do!"

Once we have created programs such as those described in this book, we may need to create teams that allow them to survive. Life-Enriching classrooms and schools are likely to be struggling within school systems whose purpose is unfortunately not supportive of them. In any Domination system the goal, unwittingly or otherwise, is to perpetuate the status quo—an economic system in which a few people maintain their wealth and privilege while others remain permanently in or near poverty.

Such systems are not going to respond positively in the long-term to the kind of educational innovations that I propose. It may be possible to launch new educational programs, but unless we organize ongoing teams of people to sustain them, the schools are likely to soon revert back to their original structures and procedures.

If you read Michael Katz's books (*The Irony of School Reform in America* is one of them) you will see why. If we only try to change the educational system, we're not seeing the bigger picture. We will simply be repeating what he says reform movements have done since the beginning of public education in the United States: they create new programs that work better than the old ones, but they're gone in five years.

Katz says that the problem with such educational reformers is that they are starting from the assumption that it is only the educational system that needs reforming. They're not sophisticated politically. They see what's wrong with the schools but they don't see what's right with them, which is that they are accomplishing what they set out to accomplish: 1) to maintain a caste system (children from privileged classes come into the learning situation much better prepared and therefore much more likely to succeed), 2) to teach students to work for extrinsic rewards (to work for grades rather to examine whether what they are learning is supporting their lives, so that later they will work for salaries), and above all 3) to maintain the vision of obedience to authority.

Ask as many teachers as I have, "What's the basic way you are evaluated?" and they answer, "Quiet classrooms. Order in the classroom." That's the number one objective, and second is, "Attractive bulletin boards." Lately we have heard the cry for more accountability, for improved proficiency test scores, but the majority opinion is still that this goal can be accomplished only in quiet classrooms with attractive bulletin boards.

So all reformers, regardless of their educational philosophy, have been evaluating school programs from the perspective of educators. Lacking a political perspective, they failed to see that public education in the United States was established to educate people to adjust and conform to the Domination economic and governmental organizations that controlled the schools. Any reform that does not recognize this underlying truth is not likely to succeed.

The importance of building a team whose function was to sustain a Life-Enriching School was evident in a school project in which I was involved in Rockford, Illinois. It was the first time I had the opportunity to contribute to the creation of a Life-Enriching School.

As I described in the introduction, a visionary and courageous principal and superintendent of schools dreamed of creating such a school as a pilot project to demonstrate its advantages over more traditional ones. Then having shown its effectiveness, the plan was to create Life-Enriching Schools throughout the school system.

Shortly after the school project was initiated resistance to it arose. The community was not used to a school based on such values. The superintendent and principal were frequent subjects of harsh criticism and attempts were made to get them to resign. Fortunately the project was able to continue because a team of parents and teachers organized to support the superintendent in his project. I was invited by the team to offer training to the teachers and to the team of parents to support their efforts.

By educational standards, the school was highly successful. Academic achievement increased, vandalism and other forms of school violence decreased. Yet, in spite of the school being successful, four people were elected to the next school board who campaigned to get rid of the school. The people in the community were apparently unable to understand a school functioning so radically differently than the schools they had attended.

The team of parents that worked to support the creation of the school now saw that it would be necessary to continue working together to sustain the school. They planned a meeting with the school board, in the hopes of helping them better understand the principles of the school.

It wasn't easy for the team to arrange the meeting. It took ten months. The president of the board refused to answer telephone messages from the team or respond to letters. Fortunately a member of the team knew a woman who was in the same social circle as the president of the board. The parents explained the school to this woman and she was subsequently successful in getting the president of the board to arrange the proposed meeting. And the meeting achieved its desired result: the board agreed to sustain the school even though they had been elected by campaigning to get rid of it. But without the team of supportive parents, the school would surely have perished.

I was at that meeting. One of the board members, a physician, a well-educated man, and I were trying to get clear about why he was so upset about the school. He told me he had been disturbed by his observation that "The kids went from classroom to classroom but not lined up with the teacher leading." I asked for another example, and he added, "In one of the classrooms I saw the kids playing a game." And then he said some words that I have heard over and over again throughout the years. He said, "Schools are not for enjoyment. You can't learn anything if you're just playing and having fun." It was so different from what he had understood schools to be. It took some understanding on both our parts to reach the point where he was willing to support this different sort of school.

Transforming Our Schools

Though the road to educational innovation is not easy, I see it as a powerful way to ever achieve peace on this planet. If future generations can be educated in schools structured so that everyone's needs are valued, I believe they will be better able to create Life-Enriching families, work places, and governments.

There are many resources in our society that support individuals in their efforts to transform their lives. I would suggest to you that schools and other organizations can be similarly transformed— through the process and underlying principles of Nonviolent Communication. We can create a Life-Enriching system where all of us are given the chance to do what at heart we enjoy more than anything else: making life more wonderful for ourselves and others, meeting each others' needs. No matter what has happened in the past in a school or school system, if students and teachers and parents and administrators learn to connect in a Life-Enriching way, it is inevitable that they will start to create Life-Enriching communities.

I have seen it happen, time and again, and when it does it's too beautiful for words.

Bibliography

Albert, Linda. *Cooperative Discipline.* Circle Pines, MN: American Guidance Service, 1996.

Albom, Mitch. *Tuesdays with Morrie.* Doubleday, New York, 1997.

Bebermeyer, Ruth. "I Wonder" (LP album). La Crescenta, CA: Center for Nonviolent Communication, 1971.

Bebermeyer, Ruth. "Given To". La Crescenta, CA: Center for Nonviolent Communication, , 1972.

Benne, Kenneth D. "Authority in Education," in *Harvard Educational Review.* Vol. 40, No. 3. Cambridge, MA, August 1970.

Bernanos, George. Quoted in *Civil Disobedience: Theory and Practice.* Hugo Adam Bedon, ed. New York: Pegasus, 1969.

Buber, Martin. *A Believing Humanism: My Testament,* 1902-1965. New York: Simon and Schuster, 1967.

Child Development Project. "Start the Year." San Ramon, CA: Developmental Studies Center, 1991.

I like the way the Child Development Project describes the classroom as a community. They say it is a place where "care and trust are emphasized above restrictions and threats, where unity and pride (of accomplishment and in purpose) replace winning and losing, and where each person is asked, helped, and inspired to live up to such ideals and values as kindness, fairness, and responsibility. [Such] a classroom community seeks to meet each student's need to feel competent, connected to others, and autonomous. Students are not only exposed to basic human values, they also have many opportunities to think about, discuss, and act on these values, while gaining experiences that promote empathy and understanding of others."

Child Development Project. "Ways We Want Our Class to Be: Class Meetings That Build Commitment to Kindness and Learning." Oakland, CA: Developmental Studies Center, 1996.

Instead of creating concrete rules, this project suggests discussions about the "ways we want our class to be" and how that can be made to happen.

Chuang Tzu, *The Way of Chuang Tzu.* N.p., n.d.

Clark, Edward T. Jr. *Designing and Implementing An Integrated Curriculum.* Brandon, VT: Holistic Education Press, 1997.

Clark advocates a functional literacy in which "teachers and students are working cooperatively to insure that every student who graduates is functionally literate, that is, they are prepared to respond deliberately and creatively to the demands of economic necessity, enlightened and informed social responsibility, and qualified planetary citizenship." (p. 51) "functional literacy must include the capacity to consciously and deliberatively create personal and collective visions of desired futures and the competencies necessary to make those futures manifest." (p. 52) In discussing operating principles for living systems, Clark states, "Interdependence is the unifying principle operative in all systems. As the first principle of ecology, it defines the nature of the complex web of relationships that exist among the individual parts of a system and between those parts and the system as a whole. (p. 100) "Interdependence is a universal characteristic recognized as being fundamental to the success of all social, economic, and political systems. Once a child understands what interdependence means, he or she is able, through the transfer of learning, to operationalize the concept in a virtually limitless number of applications." (p. 101)

Clark, Kenneth. *Dark Ghetto.* New York: Harper & Row, 1965.

Combs, Arthur W. "Seeing is Believing." ASCD Annual Conference Address, 1958.

Covaleskie, John, F. "Discipline and Morality: Beyond Rules and Consequences." *Educational Forum,* 1992. vol. 56, 173-183.

"A program that teaches children that they are expected to obey rules, even legitimate and properly established rules, fails the children and the larger society." Dalai Lama, Message from the Dalai Lama, Central Tibetan Administration, Department of Information and International Relations, 2000.

Along with education, which generally deals only with academic accomplishments, we need to develop more altruism and sense of caring and responsibility for others in the minds of the younger generation studying in various educational institutions. This can be done without necessarily involving religion. One could therefore call this 'secular ethics', as it in fact consists of basic human qualities such as kindness, compassion, sincerity and honesty.

Deci, E.L., and Richard Ryan. *Intrinsic Motivation and Self-Determination in Human Behavior*. New York: Plenum, 1985.

Rewards are just "control through seduction."

Dennison, George. *The Lives of Children*. New York: Random House, 1969.

DeVries, Rheta, and Betty Zan. *Moral Classrooms, Moral Children: Creating a Constructivist Atmosphere in Early Education*. New York: Teachers College Press, 1994.

In this book the authors express that children must actively come to their own awareness of ethical meaning.

Dewey, John. *Experience and Education*. New York: Collier Books, 1938.

Eisler, Riane. *The Chalice and the Blade*. San Francisco: Harper & Row, 1987.

Riane Eisler is a member of the General Evolution Research Group, the World Academy of Art and Science, and the World Commission on Global Consciousness and Spirituality. She is President of the Center for Partnership Studies (www.partnershipway.org)

Eisler, Riane. *The Power of Partnership*. Novato, CA: New World Library, 2002.

Winner of the 2003 Nautilus Award.

Eisler, Riane. *Tomorrow's Children*. Boulder, CO: Westview, 2000.

Applies her research on the partnership and domination models to education and was selected as the top ten of the most important books on the future by the journal Futures Studies.

Ellis, Albert, and Robert A. Harper. *A Guide to Rational Living.* Hollywood, CA: Wilshire Book Co., 1961.

Farber, Jerry. *Student as Nigger.* New York: Paperback Books, 1970.

Freire, Paulo. *Pedagogy of the Oppressed.* New York: Herder & Herder, 1971.

Fromm, Erich. *The Revolution of Hope.* New York: Bantam Books, 1968.

Gatto, John Taylor. *A Different Kind of Teacher.* Berkeley, CA: Berkeley Hills Books, 2001.

Gardner, Herb. *A Thousand Clowns.* New York: Random House, 1962.

Glazer, Steven, ed. *The Heart of Learning: Spirituality in Education.* New York: Penguin Putnam, 1999.

Gordon, Thomas. *Parent Effectiveness Training.* New York: Wyden, Inc., 1970.

Grammer, Kathy and Red Grammer. "Teaching Peace." Smilin' Atcha Music, ASCAP, 1986.

Hampden-Turner, Charles. *Radical Man.* Cambridge, MA: Schenkman Pub. Co., 1970.

Holt, John. *How Children Fail.* New York: Pittman Publishing Corp., 1964.

Howe, Ruell. *Miracle of Dialogue.* New York: The Seabury Press, 1963.

Illich, Ivan. N.r.,n.p., n.d.

Katz, Michael. *The Irony of Early School Reform: Educational Innovation in Mid-Nineteenth Century Massachusetts.* Cambridge: Harvard University Press, 1968.

Kelley, Earl C. *In Defense of Youth.* Englewood Cliffs, N. J.: Prentice-Hall, 1962.

Kohl, Herbert. *The Open Classroom.* New York: Vintage Books, 1969.

Kohn, Alfie. *Beyond Discipline: From Compliance to Community.* Alexandria, VA: Association for Supervision and Curriculum Development, 1996.

"Ethical sophistication consists of some blend of principles and caring, of knowing how one ought to act and being concerned about others." (p. 29) "Rewards, like punishments, can only manipulate someone's actions. They do nothing to help a child become a kind or caring person." (p. 34) "What we have to face is that the more we "manage" students' behavior and try to make them do what we say, the more difficult it is for them to become morally sophisticated people who think for themselves and care about others." (p 62) "In saying that a classroom or school is a 'community,' I mean that it is a place in which students feel cared about and are encouraged to care about each other." (p. 101)

Kohn, Alfie. *Punished by Rewards*, New York: Houghton-Mifflin, 1993.

Lantieri, Linda, and Janet Patti. *Waging Peace in Our Schools.* Boston: Beacon Press, 1996.

"Our society needs a new way of thinking about what it means to be an educated person. We can no longer turn away from the emotional fabric of children's lives or assume that learning can take place isolated from their feelings. We need a vision of education that recognizes that the ability to manage our emotions, resolve conflicts, and interrupt biases are fundamental skills - skills that can and must be taught." (p. 3) "We believe in a new educational model, one which includes social and emotional learning from a multicultural perspective. In this model, schools help young people become caring individuals who participate as citizens in a democratic process within a pluralistic community." (p. 7)

Mager, Robert. *Preparing Instructional Objectives.* Palo Alto, CA: Fearon Publishers, 1962.

Marshall, Max S. *Teaching Without Grades..* Corvallis: Oregon State University Press, 1968.

May, Rollo. *Man's Search for Himself.* New York: W. W. Norton & Co., 1953.

George A. Miller. "Psychology as a Means of Promoting Human Welfare." *American Psychologist*, December 1969, vol. 24, no.12.

"The most urgent problems of our world today are the problems we have made for ourselves. They have not been caused by some heedless or malicious inanimate Nature, nor have they been imposed on us as punishment by the will of God. They are human problems whose solutions will require us to change our behavior and our social institutions.

Orr, David W. *Earth in Mind: On Education, Environment, and the Human Prospect.* Washington, D.C.: Island Press, n.d.

"If today is a typical day on the planet Earth, we will lose 116 square miles of rain forest, or about an acre a second. We will lose another 72 square miles to encroaching deserts, the result of human mismanagement and over population. We will lose 40 to 250 species. It is worth noting that this is not the work of ignorant people. Rather, it is largely the results of work by people with B.A.s, B.S.s, LL.B.s, M.B.A.s, and Ph.D.s."

Piaget, Jean. *The Moral Judgment of the Child.* New York: Free Press, 1965.

"Moral autonomy appears when the mind regards as necessary an ideal that is independent of all external pressures."

Postman, Neil, and Charles Weingartner. *Teaching as a Subversive Activity.* New York: Delacorte Press, 1969.

Postman, Neil. *The End of Education: Redefining the Value of School.* New York: Vintage Books, 1996.

"We could improve the quality of schooling overnight, as it were, if math teachers were assigned to teach art, art teachers science, science teachers English. My reasoning is as follows: Most teachers, especially high school and college teachers, teach subjects they were good at in school. They found the subject both easy and pleasurable. As a result, they are not likely to understand how the subject appears to those who are not good at it, or don't care about it, or both."

Prather, Hugh. *Notes to Myself: My Struggle to Become a Person.* Lafayette, CA: Real People Press, 1970.

Raths, Louis E., Merrill Harmin, and Sidney B. Simon. *Values and Teaching*. Columbus, Ohio: Charles E. Merrill Pub. Co., 1966.

Rogers, Carl R. "Some Elements of Effective Interpersonal Communication." From speech given at California Institute of Technology, Pasadena, CA, Nov. 9, 1964.

Rogers, Carl R. "The Interpersonal Relationship in the Facilitation of Learning." in *Humanizing Education: The Person in the Process*. Edited by Robert R. Leeper. Washington, D.C.: Association for Supervision & Curriculum Development, National Education Association, 1967.

Rogers, Carl R. "What Psychology Has to Offer Teacher Education" in *Mental Health and Teacher Education*. Dubuque, Iowa: William C. Brown Co., Inc. Forty-Sixth Yearbook, 1967.

Rogers, Carl R. *Freedom to Learn*. Columbus, Ohio: Charles E. Merrill Co., 1969.

Rosenthal, Robert, and Lenore Jacobson. *Pygmalion in the Classroom: Teacher Expectations and Pupil's Intellectual Ability*. New York: Holt, Rinehart & Winston, 1968.

Sax, Saville, and Sandra Hollander. *Reality Games*. New York: Macmillan Co., 1971.

Silberman, Charles. *Crisis in the Classroom*. New York: Random House, 1970.

Tolstoy, Leo. *Tolstoy on Education*. Translated by Leo Weiner. Chicago: University of Chicago Press, 1967.

Vallet, Robert. *The Remediation of Learning Disabilities*. Belmont, CA: Fearon Publishers, 1967.

Vallet, Robert. *Programming Learning Disabilities*. Belmont, CA: Fearon Publishers, 1969.

Van Witson, Betty. *Perceptual Learning Disabilities*. New York: (Columbia) Teachers College Press, 1967.

Whitehead, Alfred North. *The Aims of Education*. New York: Free Press, 1957.

"There is only one subject matter for education, and that is Life in all its manifestations."

Willis, Mariaemma, and Victoria Kindle Hodson, *Discover Your Child's Learning Style*, Rocklin, CA: Prima Publishing, 1999.

" . . . higher level reasoning skills are achieved precisely when we allow (people) to learn through (their) strongest modality, whatever it may be." (p. 154)

Wink, Walter. *The Powers That Be.* New York: Doubleday, 1998.

Zahn-Waxler, C., M. Radke-Yarrow, E. Wagner, and M. Chapman, "Development of Concern for Others." *Developmental Psychology.* 1992. 28, 127, 135.

"Even children as young as 2 years old have (a) the cognitive capacity to interpret the physical and psychological states of others, (b) the emotional capacity to affectively experience the other's state, and (c) the behavioral repertoire that permits the possibility of trying to alleviate discomfort in others. These are the capabilities that, we believe, underlie children's caring behavior in the process of another person's distress. Young children seem to show patterns of moral internalization that are not simply fear based or solely responsive to parental commands. Rather, there are signs that children feel responsible for (as well as connected to and dependent on) others at a very young age."

Index

A

accountability vs. grades, 87–90
action language, 36–38
advising, 56
agreeing, 56, 57
Albom, Mitch, 4
altruism, as educational goal, 97–98, 107
Anderson, JoAnn, xvi–xvii, 58–59
apologizing, 56
"attention deficit disorder" diagnosis, 127
authority, respect for, 112
autonomy needs, 31

B

beanbag game incident, 47–49
Bebermeyer, Ruth, 16–18
"behavior disordered" diagnosis, 126

C

cause vs. stimulus of feelings, 29–30
celebration needs, 31
The Chalice and the Blade (Eisler), 109–10
choice factor in learning, 70–71, 81–82
Chuang-Tzu, 51
claiming understanding, 56

Clark, Kenneth, 127–28
clear action language, 36–38
community, interdependent learning, 4, 97–101
competition for rewards, 4, 98
conflict mediation with NVC, examples, 5–9, 74–76, 118–25
conflict resolution, Life-Enriching and Domination models compared, 111–12
criticism, 14, 16, 30, 61
"culturally disadvantaged" diagnosis, 126

D

Dalai Lama, 97–98
Dark Ghetto (Clark), 127–28
demands vs. requests, 38–39, 43–46
diagnoses, 30, 44, 126–28
disagreeing, 56
Domination model
choice factor in, 70–71
described, 2–3, 67–68, 109–13
language of, 11–12, 126–28
reward and punishment in, 14, 128–34
status quo perpetuation as goal, 135–36
"do-nothing room" incident, 114–18
duty, as motivator, 2–3, 113

"dysfunctional family" diagnosis, 126

E

educational resources, 101–4
Eisler, Riane, 109–10
"emotionally disturbed" diagnosis, 126, 128
empathy. *see* listening empathically
evaluation process, 11–15, 83–90
evaluation vs. observation, 16–22
explaining, 56

F

fear, as motivator, 2–3, 16, 68
feelings
    identifying and expressing, 23, 29
    needs and, 29–30
    practice exercises, 26–28
    vocabulary list of, 24–25
    see also listening empathically
    folders, student progress, 105–6
force
"for his own good", 71–72
protective vs. punitive, 4, 128–34

G

geographical community resources, 104
grades and tests, 4, 87–95

Grammer, Kathy and Red, 61
guilt, as motivator, 2–3, 16, 113

H

"hyperactive" diagnosis, 127

I

instructional materials, 101–3
integrity needs, 31
interdependence needs, 31
interdependent learning community, 4, 97–101
interpreting, 30, 56
The Irony of School Reform in America (Katz), 135–36
Israel, Life-Enriching Schools, xvii, 99, 118–19
"I've never seen a lazy man" (Bebermeyer), 16–18

J

judgments, 2, 11–15, 30, 56, 126–28, 129
justifying, 56

K

Katz, Michael, 135–36

L

labeling, 11–12, 30, 44, 128
    see also diagnoses; judgments
language
    of Domination systems, 11–12, 126–28
    of performance evaluation, 11–15

of requests, 36–38, 45
vocabulary of feeling states,
24–25
see also Nonviolent
Communication
"learning disabled" diagnosis,
126, 128
learning objectives, Domination
model, 68
learning objectives, mutually
agreed upon, 3
choice factor, 70–71, 81–82
communication skills for,
69, 74–80
evaluation process, 83–90
examples, 72–73
Life-Enriching purposes of,
68
students' fears, 82
teachers' fears, 71–72
learning units, 101–2
Life-Enriching model, described,
xviii, 1–4, 97, 107, 109,
111–13
listening empathically
vs. agreement, 57
attempts at, 55–57
with full presence, 51–52, 58
practice exercises, 63–66
for requests, 54–55
and time constraints, 57–58
for unexpressed feelings or
needs, 60–61, 74–80, 92–95
verbal reflection, 53–54, 58

M

materials, instructional, 101–3

mediation process, 5–9, 74–76,
118–25
Mildred, 58–59
Miller, George, 109
moralistic judgments, 2, 11–15,
30, 126–28, 129
motivators, 2–3, 16, 68, 113

N

needs
feelings and, 29–31
identifying, 31–32
practice exercises, 33–35, 77
Nonviolent Communication
(NVC) components
overview, 3, 15–16
feelings, identifying and
expressing, 23–29
listening empathically,
51–66
needs, identifying, 29–35
observation without
evaluating, 16–22
requests, 36–46
Nonviolent Communication
(NVC) objective, 16, 43, 76
"no" response to requests,
74–80

O

obedience vs. self-discipline,
112–13
objectives. *see* learning objectives
obligation, as motivator, 2–3, 113
observation without evaluating
overview, 16–19
examples, 18–19

practice exercises, 20–22

P

Page, Bill, xvi
paraphrasing, 57
   see also listening empathi-
     cally
parents as educational
   resources, 102–3
parroting vs. listening empathically, 58
partnership model. *see* Life-
   Enriching model
partnership relationships, in setting objectives. *see* learning
   objectives
peacemakers, 118–19
   see also mediation
performance evaluation, 11–15,
   83–90
permissiveness, 68, 118
personalizing, 56
physical nurturance needs, 31
playground conflict mediation
   incident, 5–9
play needs, 31
positive action language, 36–38
The Power of Partnership
   (Eisler), 109–10
"power-over" tactics, 67, 110–11
The Powers That Be (Wink),
   110–11
praise, 14
Prather, Hugh, 59
presence, as empathy component, 51–52, 58
probing, 56

protective use of force, 4,
   128–34
punishment and reward, 2–4,
   14, 16, 68, 113, 118
punitive use of force, 128–34

R

receiving empathically. *see* listening empathically
requests
   vs. demands, 38–39, 43–46
   listening for, 54–55
   phrasing, 36–38
   practice exercises, 40–42
   resources, educational,
     101–4
reward and punishment, 2–3,
   14, 16, 68, 113, 118, 128–34
"right"/"wrong" judgments,
   11–15
Rockford (Illinois) Life-
   Enriching Schools, xvi–xvii,
   136–38
Rogers, Carl, 81–82
rules and regulations, 4, 111, 118

S

Schwartz, Morrie, 4, 89
secular ethics, 97–98
"See Me Beautiful" (Grammer),
   61
self-discipline vs. obedience,
   112–13
Shaheen, Tom, xvi–xvii
shame, as motivator, 2–3, 16,
   113
Shapiro, Miri, xvii

silence, listening empathically
to, 60
songs, 16–18, 61
"special needs" diagnosis, 126
"spinach theory", 71–72
spiritual communion needs, 31
stimulus vs. cause of feelings,
29–30
students as teachers, 98–101
sustaining teams, 135–39
sympathizing, 52, 56

T

teacher as travel agent, 100–101
teaching units, 101–2
tests and grades, 4, 87–95
time constraints, 57–58
Tuesdays With Morrie (Albom),
4, 89

U

understanding vs. empathy, 56
units of learning, 101–2
universal human needs, 31

V

value judgments, 11–15
verbal reflection, 53–54, 58
volunteer tutoring services,
103–4

W

Wink, Walter, 110–11

Notes

Some Basic Feelings We All Have

Feelings when needs "are" fulfilled

- Amazed
- Confident
- Energetic
- Glad
- Inspired

- Joyous
- Optimistic
- Relieved
- Surprised
- Touched

- Comfortable
- Eager
- Fulfilled
- Hopeful
- Intrigued

- Moved
- Proud
- Stimulated
- Thankful
- Trustful

Feelings when needs "are not" fulfilled

- Angry
- Confused
- Disappointed
- Distressed
- Frustrated

- Hopeless
- Irritated
- Nervous
- Puzzled
- Sad

- Annoyed
- Concerned
- Discouraged
- Embarrassed
- Helpless

- Impatient
- Lonely
- Overwhelmed
- Reluctant
- Uncomfortable

Some Basic Needs We All Have

Autonomy

- Choosing dreams/goals/values
- Choosing plans for fulfilling one's dreams, goals, values

Celebration

- Celebrate the creation of life and dreams fulfilled
- Celebrate losses: loved ones, dreams, etc. (mourning)

Integrity

- Authenticity • Creativity
- Meaning • Self-worth

Interdependence

- Acceptance • Appreciation
- Closeness • Community
- Consideration
- Contribute to the enrichment of life
- Emotional Safety • Empathy

Physical Nurturance

- Air • Food
- Movement, exercise
- Protection from life-threatening forms of life: viruses, bacteria, insects, predatory animals
- Rest • Sexual expression
- Shelter • Touch • Water

Play

- Fun • Laughter

Spiritual Communion

- Beauty • Harmony
- Inspiration • Order • Peace

- Honesty (the empowering honesty that enables us to learn from our limitations)
- Love • Reassurance
- Respect • Support
- Trust • Understanding

About CNVC and NVC

2428 Foothill Blvd., Suite E, La Crescenta, CA 91214
Tel: (818) 957-9393 • Fax: (818) 957-1424
Email: cnvc@cnvc.org • Website: www.cnvc.org

The **Center for Nonviolent Communication** is a global organization whose vision is a world where everyone's needs are met peacefully. Our mission is to contribute to this vision by facilitating the creation of life-enriching systems within ourselves, inter-personally, and within organizations. We do this by living and teaching the process of Nonviolent Communication[SM] (NVC), which strengthens people's ability to compassionately connect with themselves and one another, share resources, and resolve conflicts peacefully.

CNVC is dedicated to fostering a compassionate response to people by honoring our universally shared needs for autonomy, celebration, integrity, interdependence, physical nurturance, play, and spiritual communion. We are committed to functioning, at every level of our organization and in all of our interactions, in harmony with the process we teach, operating by consensus, using NVC to resolve conflicts, and providing NVC training for our staff. We often work collaboratively with other organizations for a peaceful, just and ecologically balanced world.

Purpose, Mission, History, and Projects

What NVC Is—It is a powerful process for inspiring compassionate connection and action. It provides a framework and set of skills to address human problems, from the most intimate relationships to global political conflicts. NVC can help prevent conflicts as well as peacefully resolve them. NVC helps us to focus on the feelings and needs we all have, instead of thinking and speaking in terms of dehumanizing labels or other habitual patterns—which are easily heard as demanding and antagonistic, and which contribute to violence towards ourselves, others, and the world around us. NVC empowers people to engage in a creative dialogue in order to construct their own fully satisfactory solutions.

Where NVC Came From—Marshall B. Rosenberg first developed the NVC process in 1963 and he has been continuously refining it ever since. Rosenberg learned about violence at an early age and developed a strong desire to understand what contributed to people being violent to one another, and to explore what kind of language, thought, and communication could provide peaceful alternatives to the violence he encountered. His interest led to graduate school, where he earned a Ph.D. in clinical psychology. He first used NVC to support communities working to peacefully integrate schools and other public institutions during the 1960's. His work on these projects brought Dr. Rosenberg into contact with people in various U.S. cities who wanted to bring his training to a broad base of people in their communities. To meet this need and to more effectively spread the process of NVC, in 1984 he founded the Center for Nonviolent Communication (CNVC) and has since created many materials, including two trade edition books: *Nonviolent Communication: A Language of Life*, 2nd Edition, and *Life-Enriching Education.*

For many years the Center for Nonviolent Communication has been contributing to a vast social transformation in thinking, speaking and acting—showing people how to connect in ways that inspire compassionate results. Training in NVC is now offered throughout the world by Dr. Rosenberg and a team of more than 100 certified trainers, and is supported by hundreds of committed volunteers who help organize workshops, participate in practice groups, and coordinate team building. The training is helping prevent and resolve conflicts in schools, businesses, health care centers, prisons, community groups and families. Marshall Rosenberg and his associates have introduced NVC in war torn areas such as Sierra Leone, Sri Lanka, Rwanda, Burundi, Bosnia and Serbia, Colombia and the Middle East.

We are now seeking funds to support projects in including North America, Latin America, South America, Europe, Africa, South Asia, Brazil, and the Middle East. Foundation grants have helped launch CNVC innovative learning projects to create resources for educators, and projects that focus on parenting, social change, and prison work in various geographical regions of the world. We are working in synergy with other organizations whose missions are aligned with ours. Please visit the CNVC website for information about these projects, regional websites, and for other resources available for learning NVC. Your contribution in support of these efforts will be greatly appreciated.

A list of CNVC certified trainers and contact information for them may be found on the Center's website. This list is updated monthly. The website also includes information about CNVC sponsored trainings and links to affiliated regional websites. CNVC invites you to consider bringing NVC training to your business, school, church, or community group. For current information about trainings scheduled in your area, or if you would like to organize NVC trainings, be on the CNVC mailing list or support our efforts to create a more peaceful world, please contact CNVC.

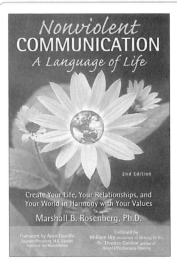

Nonviolent Communication^{SM}

A Language of Life, 2nd Edition

Marshall B. Rosenberg, Ph.D.

ISBN: 1-892005-03-4 • Trade Paper 6x9
Price: $17.95 US, $26.95 CAN
Distributed by IPG: 800-888-4741

Enjoy Powerful and Satisfying Relationships . . . in All Areas of Your Life

Most of us have been educated from birth to compete, judge, demand, diagnose—to think and communicate in terms of what is "right" and "wrong" with people. Even when we are well-meaning this can be disastrous to our relationships—both personal and professional. At best, the habitual ways we think and speak hinder communication, and create misunderstanding and frustration in others and in ourselves. And still worse, they cause anger and pain, and may lead to violence. Without wanting to, even people with the best of intentions generate needless conflict.

Nonviolent Communication helps you:

- Free yourself from the effects of past experiences and cultural conditioning
- Break patterns of thinking that lead to arguments, anger and depression
- Resolve conflicts peacefully, whether personal or public, domestic or international
- Create social structures that support everyone's needs being met
- Develop relationships based upon mutual respect, compassion, and cooperation

"Nonviolent communication is a simple yet powerful methodology for communicating in a way that meets both parties' needs. This is one of the most useful books you will ever read."
—WILLIAM URY, co-author of *Getting to Yes* and author of *The Third Side*

"This book gives people both a way of expressing their needs nonblamefully and a way of listening so others feel not just heard, but understood."
—DR. THOMAS GORDON, author, *Parent Effectiveness Training (P.E.T.)*

Available from CNVC, all major bookstores and Amazon.com
Distributed by IPG: 800-888-4741

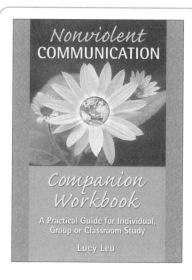

Nonviolent Communication℠ Companion Workbook

by Lucy Leu

ISBN: 1-892005-04-2 • Trade Paper 7x10
Price: $19.95 US, $29.95 CAN
Distributed by IPG: 800-888-4741

Create your life, your relationships, and your world in harmony with your values.

It's time to put Nonviolent Communication into practice, and this workbook will help you do it. Supporting you through each chapter of Rosenberg's book, this workbook contains refreshing and empowering ideas for: dealing with anger, resolving conflict, improving internal dialogue, and relating more compassionately with others.

- For **INDIVIDUALS**, this workbook provides you with activities and ideas for employing the liberating principles of NVC in your daily life.

- For **GROUP PRACTICE**, this workbook offers guidance for getting started, curriculum, and activities for each chapter.

- For **TEACHERS**, this workbook serves as the basis for developing your own courses, or to augment an existing curriculum.

LUCY LEU is the former Board President of the Center for Nonviolent Communication, and editor of the best selling *Nonviolent Communication: A Language of Life*. Currently she heads the Freedom Project, bringing NVC training to prison inmates to contribute to their reintegration into society. For information about the Freedom Project email: freedom_project@hotmail.com

Available from CNVC, all major bookstores and Amazon.com
Distributed by IPG: 800-888-4741

NVC Booklets from PuddleDancer Press

We Can Work It Out $6
Resolving Conflicts Peacefully and Powerfully   (6x9, 32 pages)
by Marshall B. Rosenberg, Ph.D. • Practical suggestions for
fostering caring, genuine cooperation, and satisfying resolutions in
even the most difficult situations.

Teaching Children Compassionately $8
How Students and Teachers Can Succeed with Mutual   (6x9, 48 pages)
Understanding • by Marshall B. Rosenberg, Ph.D.
Skills for creating a successful classroom—from a keynote address and
workshop given to a national conference of Montessori educators.

What's Making You Angry? $6
10 Steps to Transforming Anger So Everyone Wins   (6x9, 32 pages)
by Shari Klein and Neill Gibson • A step-by-step guide to
re-focus your attention when you're angry, and create outcomes that
are satisfying for everyone.

The Heart of Social Change $8
How to Make a Difference in Your World   (6x9, 48 pages)
by Marshall B. Rosenberg, Ph.D. • Marshall offers an insightful
perspective on effective social change, and how-to examples.

Parenting From Your Heart $8
Sharing the Gifts of Compassion, Connection, and Choice   (6x9, 48 pages)
by Inbal Kashtan • Addresses the challenges of parenting with real-
world solutions for creating family relationships that meet everyone's needs.

Getting Past the Pain Between Us $8
Healing and Reconciliation Without Compromise   (6x9, 48 pages)
by Marshall B. Rosenberg, Ph.D. • Learn the healing power of
listening and speaking from the heart. Skills for resolving conflicts,
healing old hurts, and reconciling strained relationships.

Available from CNVC, order from www.CNVC.org or call 800-255-7696
For more information about these booklets visit
www.NonviolentCommunication.com

The Compassionate Classroom

by Sura Hart and Victoria Kindle Hodson

Relationship Based Teaching and Learning

The Compassionate Classroom: *Relationship Based Teaching and Learning* is a long awaited resource! Two teachers with 45 years shared experience in education combine breakthrough discoveries in brain research with Marshall Rosenberg's seminal work in communication and come to a bold conclusion-when compassion thrives, so does learning.

"THE COMPASSIONATE CLASSROOM will help teachers and students practice communicating nonviolently. Its message is crucially important, and its activities provide both fun and instruction."

> —NEL NODDINGS, author, *Educating Moral People*
> and *Starting at Home: Caring and Social Policy*

"THE COMPASSIONATE CLASSROOM presents clear and concise explanations of the 'how' and 'why' of Nonviolent Communication along with playful exercises and games that animate the joy of natural giving. I am confident that "The Compassionate Classroom" will inspire many students in my college classes to share NVC in their own classrooms and beyond."

—MICHAEL DREILING, Sociology Professor and author, University of Oregon

"THE COMPASSIONATE CLASSROOM has great exercises and practical lessons that give educators tools to implement Nonviolent Communication in the classroom and create connections with students that will enhance both learning and teaching."

—LESLIE TROOK, principal, A.P. Giannini Middle School, San Francisco, CA

Available from the Center for Nonviolent Communication
800-255-7696 and www.CNVC.org

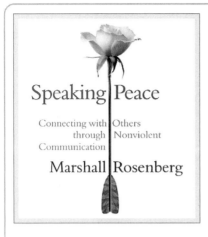

NONVIOLENT COMMUNICATION MATERIALS

Available from CNVC at www.CNVC.org or call 800-255-7696

The Compassionate Classroom $18
Relationship Based Teaching and Learning   (7.5x9, 187 pages)
by **Sura Hart and Victoria Kindle Hodson, M.A.** • This new book provides
an overview of the NVC process and its relationship to successful teaching and learning,
and specific examples of how NVC can be used in elementary school classrooms includes
playful exercises, lesson plans, and skill-building activities and games.

Raising Children Compassionately $6
Parenting the Nonviolent Communication Way   (24 pages)
by **Marshall B. Rosenberg, Ph.D.** • This booklet, filled with insights and stories,
will prove invaluable for parents, teachers and others who want to nurture children and
also themselves.

The Giraffe Classroom $18
by **Nancy Sokol Green** • Humorous, creative, and   (8.5x11, spiral bound, 122 pages)
thought provoking activities. Ideal for teachers, parents, and anyone who wants to use
concrete exercises to learn the process of NVC.

The Mayor of Jackal Heights $10
by **Rita Herzog and Kathy Smith** • A boy mayor   (8.5x11, spiral bound, 122 pages)
begins to learn how to tame his town full of jackals with the help of his wise friend,
Giraffe. A beautifully illustrated story for children of all ages.

A Model for Nonviolent Communication $8
by **Marshall B. Rosenberg** • A handbook describing the basics   (5.5x8.5, 56 pages)
of Nonviolent Communication, including exercises to help readers check their
understanding of the process. Updated, expanded, and revised.

Duck Tales and Jackal Taming Hints $4
by **Marshall B. Rosenberg, Ph.D.** • A whimsical tale about skills   (7x9, 28 pages)
needed to understand human beings, even when their communication makes them
sound like deranged jackals.

Communication Basics $4
An Overview of Nonviolent Communication   (24 pages)
by **Rachelle Lamb** • This new booklet provides a clear, concise, and handy summary
of what one might learn in an introductory training in Nonviolent Communication.

The Spiritual Basis of Nonviolent Communication $2
A Question and Answer Session with   (8.5x11, 8 pages)
Marshall Rosenberg, Ph.D. • Las Bases Espirituales De La Communicacion No
Violenta—Spanish language version available at same price.

Audiotapes, CDs, and Videotapes

Introduction To A Model for Nonviolent Communication $10
by **Marshall B. Rosenberg, Ph.D.** • Marshall Rosenberg introduces   (Audio, 90 min.)
a model for Nonviolent Communication through discussion, stories, and music.

Connecting Compassionately $10
by Marshall B. Rosenberg, Ph.D. • Workshop presentation by   (Audio, 90 min.)
Marshall Rosenberg explains the NVC process for dealing with frustrations and blocks
in communications.

Expressing and Receiving Anger $10
by Marshall B. Rosenberg, Ph.D. • How to use the principles of   (Audio, 90 min.)
Nonviolent Communication to fully express and receive anger.

Nonviolent Communication for Educators $10
by Marshall B. Rosenberg, Ph.D. • Keynote address to the   (Audio, 90 min.)
National Conference of Montessori Educators—will be of special interest to teachers,
parents and anyone who works with children.

A Heart to Heart Talk • by Marshall B. Rosenberg, Ph.D. $10
Workshop presentation at the National Conference of Montessori Educators, (Audio, 90 min.)
offers an in-depth exploration of Nonviolent Communication in the field of education.

Speaking Peace • by Marshall B. Rosenberg, Ph.D. .... 2 CD set: $25
This recording, produced by Sounds True, explains the purpose .... 2 Audio set: $20
of NVC, how to use the 4 components of the NVC model to express ourselves   (2.5 hrs.)
honestly and respond empathically to others, and to bring about change within
ourselves, others, and within larger social systems; includes songs, stories and examples.

The Basics of Nonviolent Communication $50
An Introductory Training   (2 videotapes, 3 hrs)
by Marshall B. Rosenberg, Ph.D. • This edited one-day training shows how we
can connect with others in a way that enables everyone's needs to be met through
natural giving.

Making Life Wonderful $145
An Intermediate Training   (4 videotapes, over 8 hours)
by Marshall B. Rosenberg, Ph.D. • Improve relationships with self and others
by increasing fluency in NVC. Two-day training session in San Francisco filled with
insights, examples, extended role-plays, stories, and songs that will deepen your
grasp of NVC.

About the Author

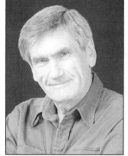

Photo by Beth Banning

MARSHALL B. ROSENBERG, PH.D. is Founder and Director of Educational Services for the Center for Nonviolent Communication (CNVC).

Growing up in a turbulent Detroit neighborhood, Dr. Rosenberg developed a keen interest in new forms of communication that would provide peaceful alternatives to the violence he encountered. His interest led to a Ph.D. in clinical psychology from the University of Wisconsin in 1961. His subsequent life experience and study of comparative religion motivated him to develop Nonviolent Communication (NVC).

Dr. Rosenberg first used NVC in federally funded projects to provide mediation and communication skills training during the 1960s. He founded the Center for Nonviolent Communication (CNVC) in 1984. Since then CNVC has grown into an international nonprofit organization with over 100 trainers. They provide training in 30 countries in North and South America, Europe, Asia, the Middle East, and Africa, and offer workshops for educators, counselors, parents, health care providers, mediators, business managers, prison inmates and guards, police, military personnel, clergy, and government officials.

Dr. Rosenberg has initiated peace programs in war torn areas including Rwanda, Burundi, Nigeria, Malaysia, Indonesia, Sri Lanka, Sierra Leone, the Middle East, Colombia, Serbia, Croatia, and Northern Ireland. Funded by UNESCO, the CNVC team in Yugoslavia has trained tens of thousands of students and teachers. The government of Israel has officially recognized NVC and is now offering training in hundreds of schools in that country.

Dr. Rosenberg is currently based in Wasserfallenhof, Switzerland, and travels regularly offering NVC training and conflict mediation.